Finance for Non-Financiers 1

Finance for Non-Financiers 1

Basic Finances

José Saul Velásquez Restrepo

Copyright © 2011 by José Saul Velásquez Restrepo.

Library of Congress Control Number: 2010939637
ISBN: Hardcover 978-1-6176-4240-1
Softcover 978-1-6176-4242-5
Ebook 978-1-6176-4241-8

All rights reserved. No part of this book may be reproduced or transmitted in any form or by any means, electronic or mechanical, including photocopying, recording, or by any information storage and retrieval system, without permission in writing from the copyright owner.

The information, ideas, and suggestions in this book are not intended to render professional advice. Before following any suggestions contained in this book, you should consult your personal accountant or other financial advisor. Neither the author nor the publisher shall be liable or responsible for any loss or damage allegedly arising as a consequence of your use or application of any information or suggestions in this book.

This book was printed in the United States of America.

To order additional copies of this book, please contact:
Palibrio
1663 Liberty Drive
Suite 200
Bloomington, IN 47403
Tel: 877.407.5847
Fax: +1.812.355.1576
Orders@Palibrio.com

Contents

Introduction 7

Chapter 1. Basic Concepts of Financial Mathematics 9

Chapter 2. Supposed Basic to Study Finances 22

Chapter 3. Financial Function 27

Chapter 4. Analysis of the Countable Principles 37

Chapter 5. Handling Cash-Electronic Bank 43

Chapter 6. Administration of Portfolio 53

Chapter 7. How to Define the Granting of Credit (method of josavere) 62

Chapter 8. Practical Aspects of the Handling of Inventories 73

Chapter 9. Model of Inventories 84

Chapter 10. Working Capital 90

Chapter 11. Financial Analysis 95

Chapter 12. State of Sources and Applications of Funds 110

INTRODUCTION

I have written this book with the aim to make easier that apparently is difficult and with the desire of contribute in the formation of a theory applicable in real life. This is a description available to everyone, though this could hardly be called a lack of depth in any of the items, which makes the text highly recommended for non-financial executives.

The approach is very practical; based on a great deal of evidence to avoid any situation that may arise in the business world and apply personal finances too. The papers are presented according to the recommended order of learning and practical exercises are made in Excel.

It is an effort that I have enthusiastically encouraged by many friends, who have helped me to mature and clarify concepts. There are so many that fail to list them and so I refrain from doing so to avoid being unfair by omitting any name oblivion unintentional. In all, my sincere thanks, on behalf of those who can draw some profit from this book.

josavere
josavere@une.net.co

Chapter 1

BASIC CONCEPTS OF FINANCIAL MATHEMATICS

by josavere

1. VALUE OF THE MONEY THROUGH TIME

Money is an asset that cost with the pass of time; the interest rates are received periodic (monthly, quarterly, etc.). In finances, is understood the composed interest: interests produced periodically turn automatically into capital.

Example:

If I place $1,000,000 (PV) to an interest rate (i) 3% monthly, when finishing the first period, the capital is equal to $1,030,000 and the new interest will be 3% of this number, and thus, successively.

- **PV:** initial capital
- **i:** interest rate
- **n:** number of periods (in the same ones that appears the rate)
- **FV:** value of the PV plus the gained interests

Periods:

First: $FV_1 = PV(1+i)$
Second: $FV_2 = FV_1(1+i) = P(1+i)^2$
Third: $FV_3 = FV_3(1+i) = P(1+i)^3$
N-m: $FV_n = FV(n-1)(1+i) = PV(1+i)^n$

KEY FOR THE ANALYSIS:

To correctly process a graph that indicates the investments (↓) and the outcome (↑) in the exact date that are considered display.

Using Excel is possible to solve any situations that may appear.

2. BASIC PROBLEMS

A. TO CALCULATE A FUTURE VALUE: knowing a real value now (present value), the interest rate and the number of periods (expressed in the same unit that **i** is defined).

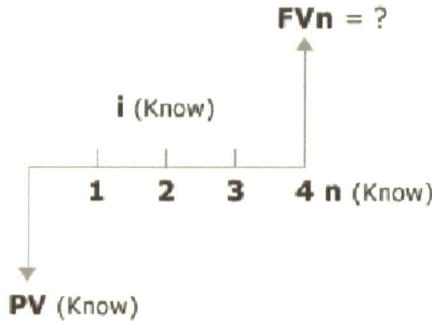

Example: PV: $1.000.000; i: 2.5%; n: 24.

$FV = PV(1+i)^n = 1000000(1+0.025)^{24} = 1.808.725,95$

Now, using Excel; steps to follow:

a. Open Excel.

b. Click in functions (fx).

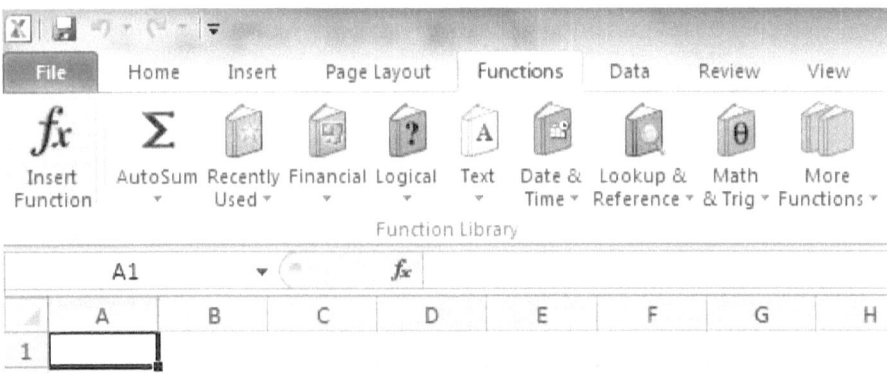

c. Select in the left menu in **"Financial"** category. In the menu of the right, it names of function **"VF"**.

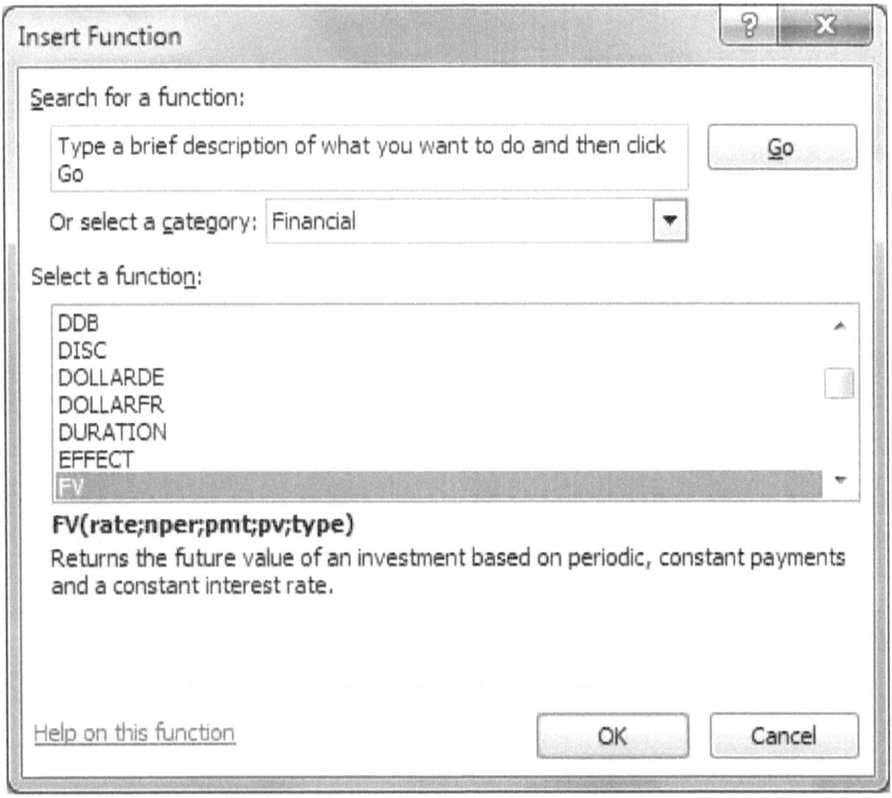

d. Click in button to accept **(it appears a window)**

e. In the box that ask for the following information:

- Interest rate(2.5%).
- Number of periods: (24).
- Payments (to place 1, in this model is unique payment).
- VA "present value" (- **1.000.000**)

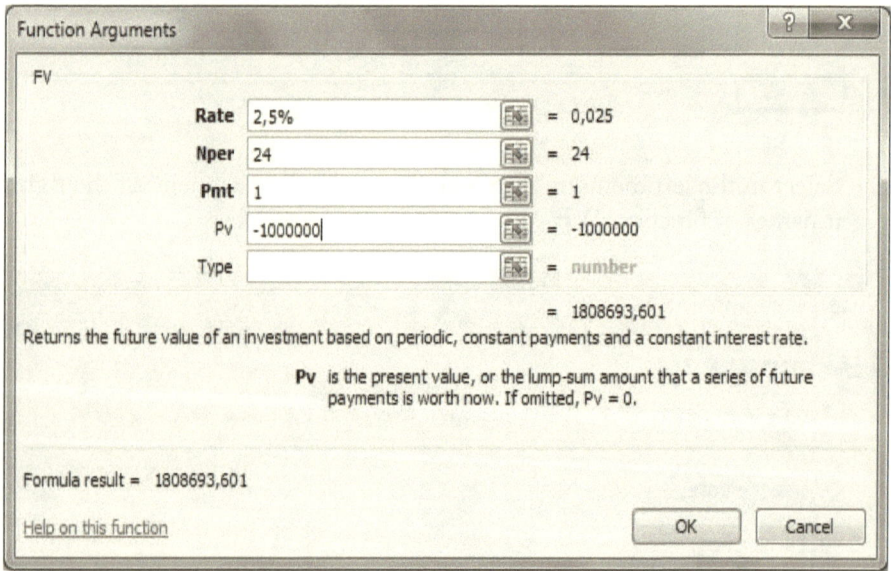

f. Click in button to accept

g. To evaluate the answer (**1.808693.601**)

B. DEFINED A FUTURE VALUE: to calculate a present value that must invest now for accumulate a sum in a defined time with a known interest rate.

Example: if I need to accumulate $5.000.000 at the end of the third year, how much money I must deposit today if 1,5% interests pay to me to monthly?

Finance for Non-Financiers 1

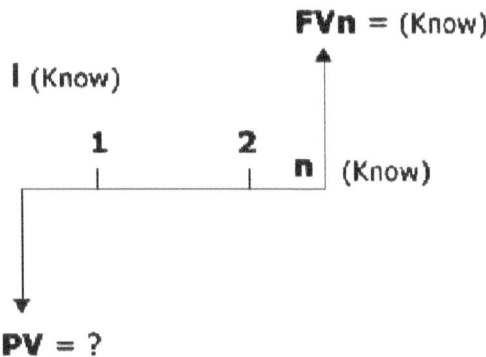

Now, calculate the same using Excel; steps to follow:

a. Open Excel.

b. Click in functions (fx).

c. Select in the left menu in **"Financial"** category. In the menu of the right, it names of function **"VF future value"**.

d. Click in button to accept **(it appears a window)**.

e. In the box that ask for the following information:

- Interest rate (1.5%).
- Number of periods: (36).
- Payments (to place 1, in this model is unique payment).
- VA "present value" (**5.000.000**)

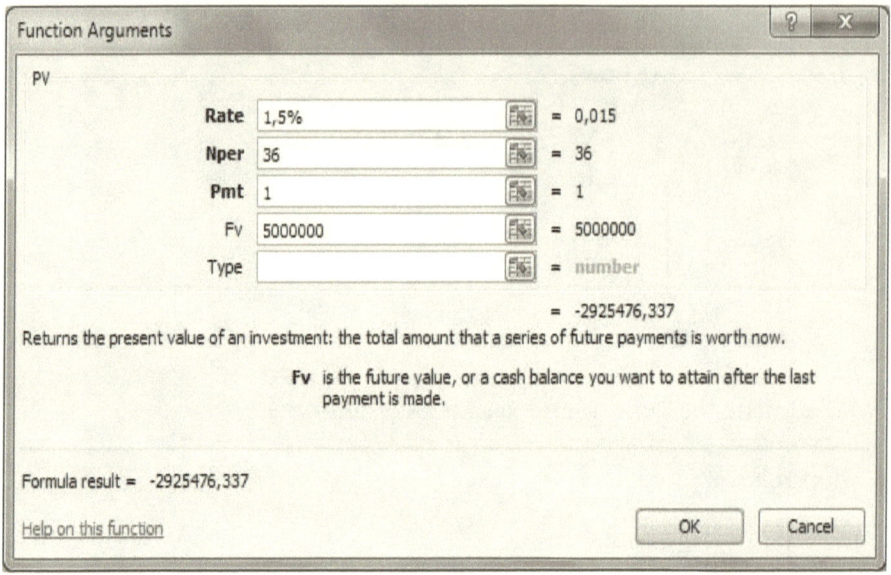

f. Click in button to accept

g. To evaluate the answer (- **2.925.476.337**)

C. TO CALCULATE THE FUTURE VALUE (FV) WITH PERIODIC PAYMENTS:

One appears when equal and periodic payments become (payments), knows the number of periods (n) and the interest rate by every period.

Example: if saving monthly a defined number, to one appraises previously agreed, during a number of periods decided how much money I reach to reunite?

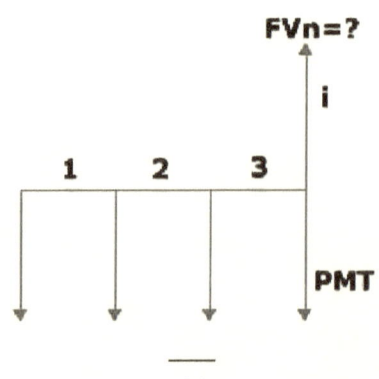

Finance for Non-Financiers 1

Numerical exercise: what capital will be at the end of 15 months, if monthly $50,000 is deposited in an investment that recognizes 1,5% by month?

Now, using Excel; steps to follow:

a. Open Excel.

b. Click in functions (fx).

c. Select in the left menu in **"Financial"** category. In the menu of the right, the function **"VF future value"**.

d. Click in button to accept **(it appears a window)**.

e. In the box that ask for the following information:

- Interest rate (1.5%).
- Number of periods: (15).
- Payments (**50.000**)

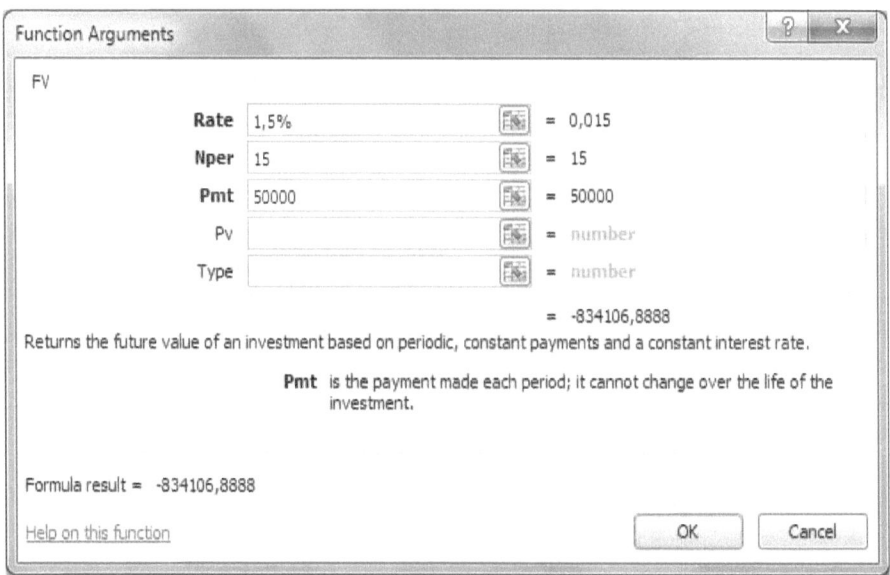

f. Click in button to accept.

g. To evaluate the answer (**- 834.106.8888**)

D. TO CALCULATE THE PERIODIC PAYMENTS (PMT): when is wanted to accumulate a future value (well-known), is defined a period of time to make it (n) and the interest rate (i), expressed in the same period of the schedule, how much one must contribute each pay?

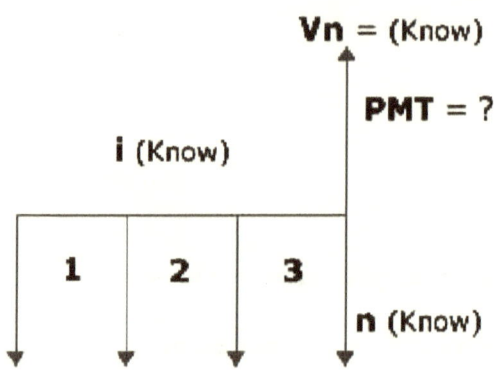

Example: how much I must save during 10 months to have $1.500.000 in the end, if they offer an interest to me of the 1,5% monthly cash.

Now, we calculate the same, but using Excel, steps to follow:

a. Open Excel.

b. Click in functions (fx).

c. Select in the left menu in **"Financial"** category. In the menu of the right, the function **"VF"**.

d. Click in button to accept **(it appears a window)**.

e. In the box that ask for the following information:

- Interest rate (1.5%).
- Number of periods: (10).
- Future value: (1.500.000) (number to accumulate)

Finance for Non-Financiers 1

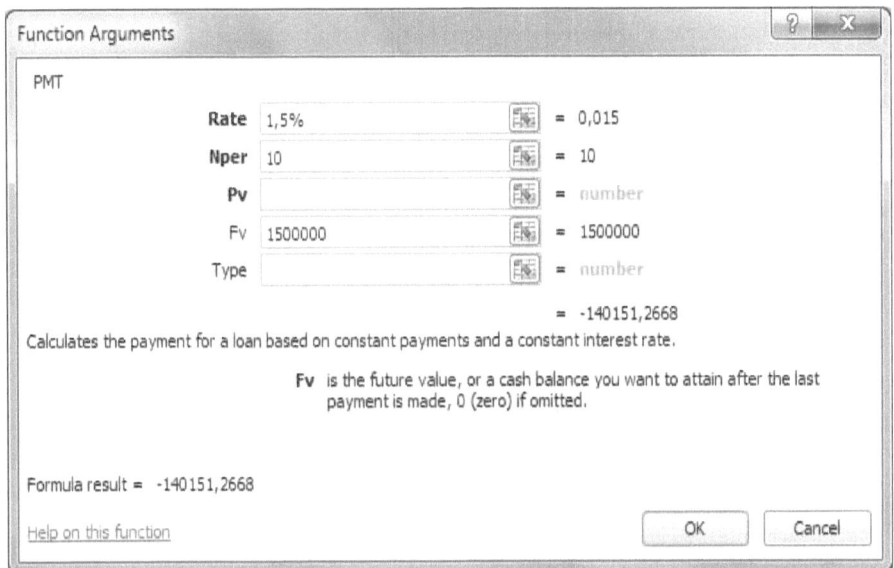

f. Click in button to accept.

g. To evaluate the answer (- **2.925.476.337**)

E. TO CALCULATE A PRESENT VALUE (PV) OF PERIODIC PAYMENTS:

To calculate a present value (PV) that gain interest rate(i), which allows receiving a defined periodic sum (well-known), during a previously decided time. If, I want to receive a monthly amount previously defined (n); the interest rate suitable, how much must give today?

Example: in order to have a rent of $500,000 monthly, during 60 months, which must be the initial investment, if the interests are recognized by month is 1,5%?

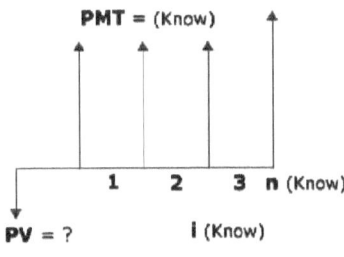

Steps to follow:

a. Open Excel.

b. Click in functions (fx).

c. Select in the left menu in **"Financial"** category. In the menu of the right, take **"Payment"**.

d. Click in button to accept **(it appears a window)**.

e. In the box that ask for the following information:

- Interest rate: (1.5%)
- Number of periods: (60)
- Future value: 500.000 (number to accumulate)

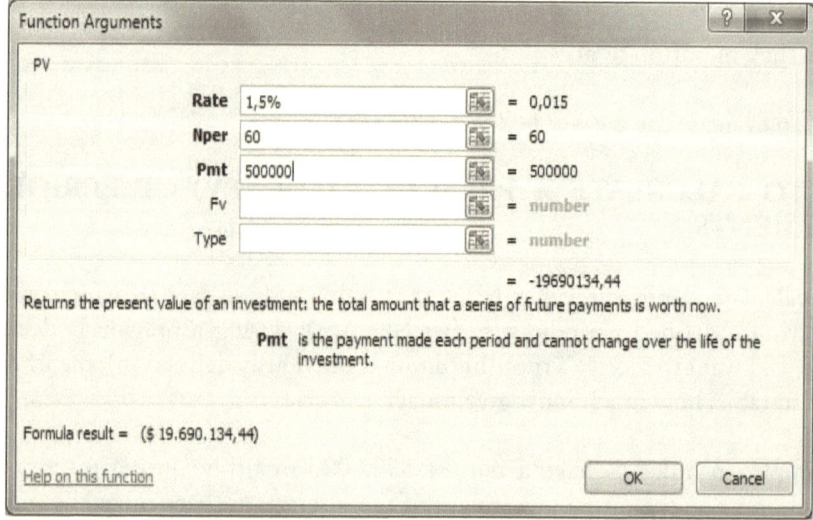

f. Click in button to accept.

g. To evaluate the answer (- **19.690.134.44**)

F. TO CALCULATE INTEREST RATE AND THE PERIODS: knowing the other elements: periodic payments, number of periods, interest rate and a present or future value, according to the case. Using the computer or the Excel, the **i** (interest rate) and the **n** can be found (periods).

Finance for Non-Financiers 1

Let us illustrate of once with examples:

I. Interest rate: as it is the interest rate that duplicates 1.000.000 of pesos in 24 months.

Steps to follow:

a. Open Excel.

b. Click in functions (fx).

c. Select in the left menu in **"Financial"** category. In the menu of the right, it names of function **"Rate"**.

d. Click in button to accept **(it appears a window)**.

e. In the box that ask for the following information:

    - Interest rate (1.5%)
    - Number of periods (24)
    - VA (- **1.000.000**)
    - VF (**2.000.000**)

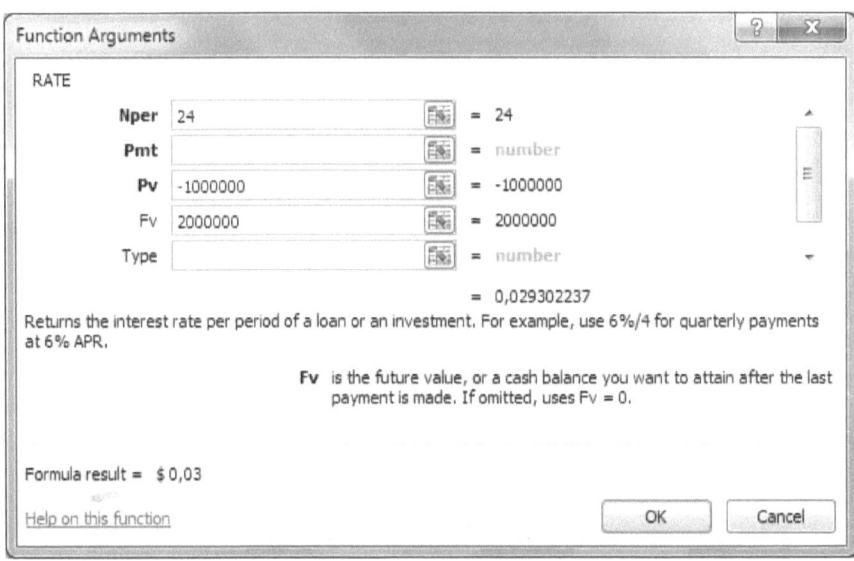

f. Click in button to accept.

19

g. To evaluate the answer (**2.9302237%**)

II. To calculate the number of periods: as soon as time I accumulate 2.000.000 dollars, investing 1.000.000 to r = 2,9302237% the monthly one.

Steps to follow:

a. Open Excel.

b. Click in functions (fx).

c. Select in the left menu in **"Financial"** category. In the menu of the right, it names of function **"Nper"** that it means I number of periods.

d. Click in button to accept **(it appears a window)**.

e. In the box that ask for the following information:

- Interest rate (2.9302237%)
- VA (- **1.000.000**)
- VF (**2.000.000**)

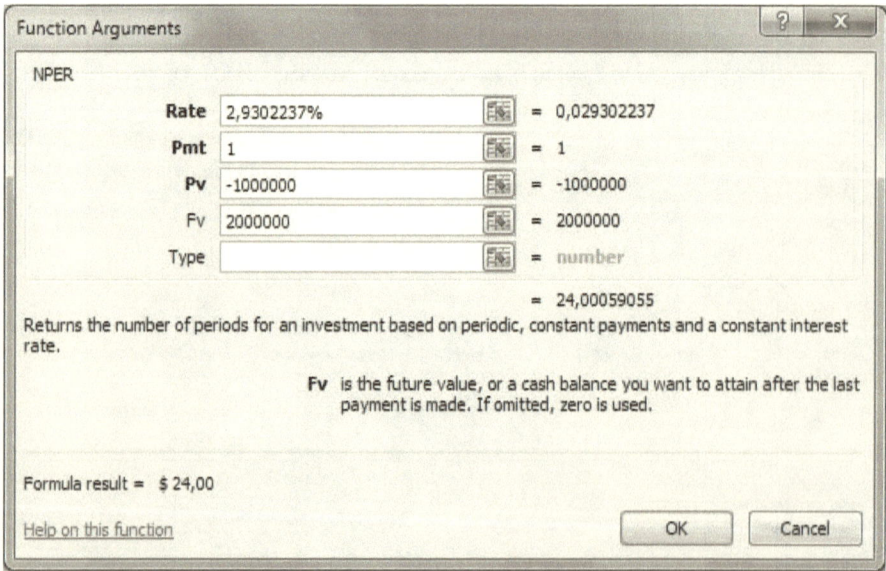

f. Click in button to accept.

g. To evaluate the answer **24 months**.

G. FORMULA TO CALCULATE THE EFFECTIVE RATE OF INTEREST

$$i_e = [1 + i/n]^n - 1$$

[Excel Function Arguments dialog box for EFFECT:
- Nominal_rate: ,12 = 0,12
- Npery: 12 = 12
- = 0,12682503
- Returns the effective annual interest rate.
- Npery is the number of compounding periods per year.
- Formula result = 0,12682503]

i_e: Effective interest rate
i: Nominal interest rate
t: Periods of capitalization

Example: if the nominal rate is of annual 36% with quarterly capitalization, how much is the effective interest?

- t: 4 trimesters
- i_e: $(1 + 0.36 / 4)^4 - 1$
- i_e: $(1 + 0.009)^4 - 1$
- i_e: 1.411582 - 1 = 0.411582
- i_e: **41.1582%**

Chapter 2

SUPPOSED BASIC TO STUDY FINANCES

by josavere

Finances constitute a fundamental element understanding and offering judging elements to facilitate the analytical approach that must be prioritized in the study of these techniques, which are made enormously possible with the use of the computers.

1. VALUE OF THE MONEY IN FUNCTION OF THE TIME

Concept explained in financier mathematics, where one assumes that all dollars generated as rent constitutes so on in a greater value of the capital and, based on the interest rate and the regularity of liquidation. The effective rate of yield will be while the shorter the period is used to pay the interests.

Using the financial mathematics we can equate an amount to receive in a future determined by that could receive in return an immediate way. The fairness depends on the rate of interest, which is agreed upon between the parties.

2. PAYMENT OF TAXES

The companies work under the jurisdiction of a country. To the government corresponds to generate the infrastructure and to create the investment climate that require the businesses; for that reason collects and redistributes

While they contribute to the companies is more efficient, the government will improve the quality of life of the inhabitants and make the country more attractive for the foreign investment, so desired as capital source.

The businessman must consider the government as the special partner and to pay of taxes and to analyze the decisions, based on structured affluent calculations.

3. YIELD AND RISK

While the greater the risk the investor must assume, the greater expectation of profit that appears will have to be; otherwise, he will look for another horizon.

As a general principle, all investment implies a risk in a greater or smaller quantity, and is very difficult to measure in quantitative terms, in spite of the great advances obtained, and measured by its degree of acceptance in the financial world. In practice, the handling of the risk requires a high dose of **individual criterion** combined with the probabilistic models. After the fall of the twin towers in New York (September 11 of 2001) is required to revalue a concept that prevailed for a long time: zero risk, a treasury bond of the U.S.A.

4. THE BENEFITS FOR THE SHAREHOLDER MUST BE TANGIBLE

This means that the results obtained by the companies must be concentrated in the value of the share in the market and a good possibility of negotiation (stock-exchange); it must be sufficiently attractive so that it generates a demand that allows the shareholder a change of investment when they wishes it, (mobility of factors). This is obtained wit properly specific information; simple, ample and transparent certified by an organization that generates credibility. It must be governed by the practice of the good corporative government.

5. CASH FLOW—SUPREME MEASURE

The benefits are tangible and the companies are attractive if pay dividends independently of the practice used to do it. Its payment implies to take care of the high-priority obligations that means: governmental, labors, operation, suppliers and the financial organizations. Even though, the cash flow discounted not always is the method adapted in valuation of companies, it constitutes the generalized tool. More important than the sale on credit, is the collection of the portfolio. The sales by cash constitute the ideal in normal conditions. The liquidity with an adapted structure of assets and an efficient administration generates yield which as well provides feedback to the liquidity and so on.

6. STUDY OF ALTERNATIVES BY CASH FLOW

Consequently with the previous assumption, evaluating a projected by cash Flow; the initial situation must be simulated and the new one (including the income and debits of cash of the project to evaluate) and later settles down the difference between the new cash flow and the initial. If the treasury situation improves the project is viable; otherwise it is rejected.

All the projects are subordinated to the *plan of generation of value* of the company; they evaluate based on the *capital cost* (dynamic concept) and the consequences of a possible cannibalism in the income are avoided.

7. PERMANENT COMPETITION

The competition is a constant in the world of businesses and seen it increased by the phenomenon of the globalization, which makes the situation every day more difficult.

The excessively **profitable businesses** are very few; in this event, they last just a short time, because quickly attract new competitors. It is important to take advantage the maximum of the competitive advantages that the moment offers, while the new actors come to complicate the business and to reduce its yield. It is fundamental to use benchmarking in consistent form as a tool of evaluation and continuous improvement.

8. OWNERS AND ADMINISTRATORS

In many cases the owners delegate the direction to other people and not always the interests of the administration are with it.

Now days the human resources is considered to the intellectual capital as the most valuable resource of the companies and to a large extent is constituted by the director's team on which the company does not have property.

The salary of risk, expectation that appears, based on the plan of value generation that must be approved by the owners (through the board of directors) constitute an excellent mechanism to make an agreement the interests of the owners and the administrators and to avoid this type of conflicts.

9. ACCOUNTING NORMS

The finances use as a basic tool, the accounting, which is not governed by *universal accounting* principles. For benchmarking effects the pertinent adjustments are required to make the financial statements comparable. The world needs to legislate on that matter before the phenomenon of the globalization settles in thus facilitating the analysis of investments.

The measurement of the possible thing, when analyzing financial statements, we must resort to a UNIQUE PLAN OF ACCOUNTS and the sector analysis.

10. SHORT AND LONG TERM HANDLING

Concept of the highest manages responsibility for board of directors is the handling of the long term. It implies a high dose of responsibility; not to show apparent profits in the short term, sacrificing the future growth and the predominant generation of value with liquidity, elements to value a company.

The cash flow generates must allow sufficient **appropriations** to finance the positioning; the qualification of *the human resource;* investment in investigation and development; the preservation of the environment and the certifications of quality. Decisions like the modernization of the equipment, the preventive maintenance, accelerated depreciation specially when one works with advanced technology, the sufficient retention of profits to withstand the inflation and to finance the growth; the care of the principle of financial conformity, constitutes a very representative example that illustrate the balance between the handling of the short and the long term.

11. CLASSIFICATION OF THE RISK

The risk is inherent to the businesses that operate in the different countries. **The risk country** in general is equal for all the companies and therefore, in principle is not diversifiable. Nevertheless its dispersion with operation in other countries can be obtained. The risk of the business is diversified with operation in another type of activities, based on a correlation analysis and at first a universal saying in finances: "don't place all eggs in the same basket".

12. ETHICS IN BUSINESSES

Ethics makes relation to everything what has to do with the moral means do the correct thing. The difficult thing for the subject is what the correct thing is depends on the values of the people, the societies and the times which in the end are codified in the laws of each country.

The ethical behavior instills confidence and the confidence very specially constitutes a pillar in the companies of the XXI century; it also implies social responsibility framed in the old saying: who does not live to serve, does not deserve to live."

By subjective and the complex thing of the subject it can summarize it in a phrase of the Eastern culture: to decide always looking for inner peace[1].

---

[1] To extend the subject to see approaches HYPERLINK"../special/personal-quality.php" THE PERSONAL QUALITY

Chapter 3

FINANCIAL FUNCTION

by josavere

Four types of decisions can be taken in business: trade, personnel, production and finance. The financial area has the responsibility of the efficient administration of the funds of the company. The financial executive has to help in the study of the investments to take the more suitable decision of financing, and to make an efficient handling of the funds that are generated, looking for the increase of the company and the generation of value that allows to pay dividends and to increase the value of the share in the market.

As the result of the combination of investments and financing, a good operation generates value and as consequence the profits are going to increase. Part of profits is distributed in dividends, which maintain the attitude of the investors. Almost all the authors of finances agree in affirming that the financial basic objective consists of maximizing the value of the company, because it implies the handling of long term, not thus, maximizing the value of the profits, since these in certain cases, can be obtained sacrificing the permanence of the company.

A financial function is full, if the intrinsic value of a share and in stock-exchange increased. In some cases, the space between the internal situation and the one of the market is explained fundamentally by lack of sufficiently ample information for the investors.

If we leave the objective of maximizing the value of the company, we found procedures that facilitate this goal in damage of the apparent yield. Among other reasons, in some countries has taken to a tax direction of the accounting for the sake of reducing the payment of taxes.

Mechanisms as accelerated depreciation; the protection of portfolio, inventories and investments; the LIFO system cost; the appropriations for contingencies, etc., that really lead to decrease the profit and as obvious consequence tend to reduce the participation of the statement treasury and the distribution of profits, complemented with the retention of the profits, fit perfectly within the frame of maximizing of the value of the company through which the lawyers call hidden reserves.

If we approve the objective previously mentioned, we could affirm that the management is good because it increases the value of the company. However, we analyze that happens with the shareholder.

Like the thickness of the public (the small shareholders), it does not know east type of direction acts generally under the concept of yield, calculated according to press report, like the relation between the dividend and the value of market. Low dividends reduce yield, which decreases price of the stock as well.

In the meantime, the great shareholders that have access to the information and they dominate the financial techniques. They know that with the handling of this practice, the real value of the stock divided by the number of shares is the real value of the share. They tend to rise and, when noticing the great abyss between the intrinsic value of the share and the value of market, they try to find a great business in the purchase of shares. As consequence, the property is concentrated decreasing of step the new shares like financing source. When concentrating the property and dominating the boards of directors, is easy to lower or still to suspend the dividend in damage of the small shareholders, in addition to so many abuses that are committed using the power.

It is important to insist on the objective to maximize the value of the share in the market; let us remember that the things are worth what they pay by them, is due to look for a good index of stock-exchange, indicator of the facility or not to negotiate the share.

1. HOW TO OBTAIN THE OBJECTIVE

Until now, countable science has developed elements of measurement of a business: the earnings statement, the general balance sheet, the statement of changes in the financial situation, the statement of cash flow and the statement of changes in the equity.

But, as we can analyze in the development of other published documents, the accounting is not able to follow the rate of the business. It is very probable that a certain company practically has a made business but without formalizing and the accounting although partly corrects the deficiency in notes to the balance does not know it, in regard to the principle of accomplishment of the profit, etc.

By the great amount of emptiness that presents/displays the accounting information, the different methods to estimate as depreciation, recognition of the profit is presented; it is necessary complement the financial information with **notes to the balance, clarifying** the accounting practices in the particular case. With a good attached explanation it is had judgment elements to determine a suitable criterion of estimate that allows to consider the value of the share. In another document we took care of this subject.

It is healthy logic, the investor, of being able to do it, will calculate the net present value of the future dividends that hopes to receive, plus the considered value of distraction and will compare with the value of market of the stock. If the net value (VPN) is superior at the cost of market, buys and if no, it rejects.

$$VPN = \sum_{t=1}^{n} \frac{DF}{(1 + k)^t} + \frac{VR}{(1 + k)^n}$$

VPN > VM: buys
VPN < VM: rejects
VPN: net present value
VM: market value
DF: waited for future dividends
VR: accomplishment value
K: minimum required rate
t: period

However, if the objective of the financial function consists of maximizing the value of the share, we will try to illustrate the three types of basic decisions to obtain it.

2. INVESTMENT DECISIONS

Accounting classified the assets in three groups: currents, fixed and others. We are speaking about the left of the balance: the structure of de actives

We understand as current assets those that represent money or are susceptible to eliminate within a cycle of the business (production, marketing, and collection) in a short period of time. These are: box and banks, temporal investments, accounts to receive, and inventories.

The fixed assets are part of the assembly itself. They are not for being commercialized but for its operation by means of the combination with the working capital. Generally, it implies great investments of capital, valorized in some cases, like lands and depreciable in others like the buildings and the machinery; amortizable in other cases like patents, mines of operation.

What it is not easily classifiable as current or fixed is called, other assets. Let us remember that these are characterized by their capacity to generate cash, its claim on them, are perfect identity and being residual in case of bankruptcy.

Now we are looking for elements that allow defining the structure of the assets. Known the objective trade for a certain period of time (hopefully minimum five years), and quantified in terms of units to produce (buy) and to sell, is basic to respond to the following question: ¿What is the minimum installation absolutely indispensable to take care of it?

In this case the minimum, indicates that the plant must be structured looking for its maximum use, avoiding immobilizing assets or this of another form, treating of which there is not installed capacity different from the contemplated one in the development plan of the company. The growth must be programmed with a maximum care. It is clear that the answer to that question not always is easy, but never will be impossible. For each case will be necessary to use the corresponding indicators to respond, in the light of the technological advances, the land availability, the premises, public services, personnel, enabled and value of the pertinent investments.

If the cost of the capital is very high, we have sufficient power facilities, good transport service to the personnel, reasonable security and the sector offers abundant labor. It is recommendable to work two or three shifts analyzing the costs labor originated by the particular circumstances.

Once the questions are solved that can be done in the feasibility study, the financial calculation begins. For it, we must quantify with extreme prudence and of maximum well-taken care, the income waited in cash and the corresponding expenses to establish the net cash flow of each specific project.

For example: we say that a project could consist of working in the rented premises, with two machines A, three B, and one D, in days of three shifts, using the third part of the premises. Another alternative could be triple the machines and the physical space in a single shift.

As the most important element appears the cost of capital, based on the time of manufacture. Logically, the faster we have the merchandise available, faster we will be able to recover the costs and to obtain the profit, if the conditions of the market allow it.

Financial mathematics has developed five methods to evaluate projects, that means:

a. **Rate average of return:** it represents the relation between the averages of net profits and the investment.

Example:

Average profits in five years: $4.000

Investments: $10.000

$$\text{R.A. of Return} = \frac{4.000}{10.000} = 40\%$$

Comparing the number obtained with the required rate, it is accepted or rejected. This method is very simple. It has the great disadvantage to ignore the dates of income and debits of the cash and therefore it does not consider the value of the money in the time, limitation very hard in inflationary economies. In addition, it does not consider the risk that implies the industrial activity.

b. **Period of reimbursement:** it indicates the time (generally in years or months), that is required to recover an initial investment.

Example:

Initial investment: $100.000

Average profit year: $20.000

$$P \text{ of } R = \frac{4.000}{10.000} = 5 \text{ years}$$

Comparing with a period previously defined it is accepted or it rejected. This method also is very simple. It does not consider the income that can be obtained after the recovery of the initial investment. In addition, it does not know the dates of the cash flow and consequently it ignores the value of the money in the time.

It can be very useful to calculate investments in hard currency or for projects of very fast recovery in inflationary, as the case of businesses of season or purely occasional business.

c. **Internal rate of return:** it consists to calculate the interest rate that equals the future income and outcome programmed of cash. This number is compared with the rate of cut of the company that the directors consider like the minimum acceptable yield.

$$A_0 = \frac{A_1}{(1+t)} = \frac{A_2}{(1+t)^2} + \frac{A_n}{(1+t)^n}$$

A_0: initial investment
A_1, A_2, A_3: future cash flow
t: rate that equals the cash flows
t vs. k, being k, the rate of cut of the company

The computers facilitate the solution of this financial problem.

This method has some disadvantages: it assumes that the funds generated by the project, are reinvested to the internal rate of return during the rest of his life, which not always occurs in the reality.

d. **Net present value:** it is very similar to the previous one. This one discounts the net cash flow using required rate of return. If the sum of the discounted cash flow is equal or greater than zero, the proposal is accepted, and if not, the proposal is rejected.

$$VPN = A_0 + \frac{A_1}{(1+k)} = \frac{A_2}{(1+k)^2} + \frac{A_n}{(1+k)^n}$$

- VPN > 0: +Accept
- VPN < 0: +Reject
- VPN: +Net present value
- k: +Rate of cut
- A: +Future income

e. **Index of yield:** it is equal to the value of the future net cash flows divided by the initial payment. If the index is superior to 100, the project is acceptable.

$$IY = \frac{VPN}{I} \quad \frac{\sum_{t=1}^{n} \frac{A_i}{(1+R)^i}}{I}$$

- IY: +index of yield
- VPN: +net present value
- I: +initial investment
- A: +future income
- k: +rate of cut

Using the most recommendable method in each case, the waited for yield of the investment calculates and soon it is compared with the parameters fixed by the directors to effect to decide if the investment is recommendable or no.

With assets fixed, we entered to calculate the proportion of working capital required for a well-organized operation.

As an initial idea, we say that in cash we required the necessary money for the transactions programmed plus a reserve considered for unforeseen expenses. The amount of accounts to receives equal to the cost of the merchandise to sell proportionality to the period. The inventory of raw material, is equal the consumption for one day by the time of replacement (days) plus the reserve. In product in process, the daily requirements by the period that takes the productive process and in finished product, the amount that gives a high probability of not losing sales. The sum of the investments in cash, accounts to receive and inventories represents the investment in **working capital.**

Of this form we completed the structure of the assets, the most important of all because it does the times of leader. If we don't have a good investment, nobody would be arranged to put or, to lend its money.

In order to make the decision from investment, we must complete with the alternatives of financing for calculating if is favorable the difference between the awaited yields and the cost of financing.

3. FINANCING DECISIONS

There are related to the structure of the liabilities, that is, the right part of the balance sheet. We never due to study if investment expectation if does not have one based well, considering the risk in direct proportion to the awaited yield.

We presented as the initial recommendation devices to look for the maximum possible indebtedness in the long term (the limit places the prescribed restrictions of the different credits from promotion). The difference between the sum of the fixed assets and the minimum of current assets, except the financed part in the long term must finance with equity capital and the temporary requirements, with liabilities in the short term. (See graph).

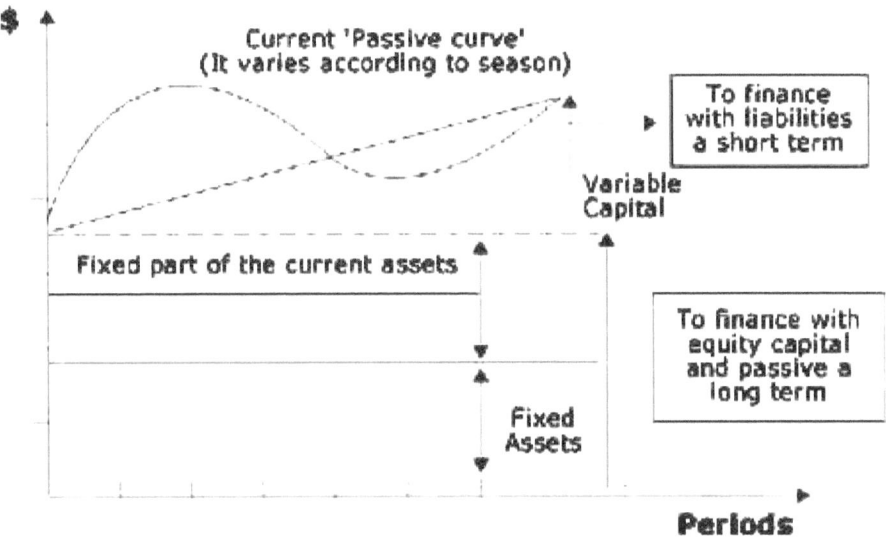

As far as lines of credit the ceaseless search of the alternatives will be the function of the financial manager that appears because these continuously change, in agreement with the economic situation and the governmental decisions. It will have to maintain updated the calculation the cost of capital permanently (dynamic concept), as it bases to verify if the company **generates value** or if it destroys it, in order to correct the situation.

The equity capital can be obtained by stock and retention of profits, as long as the investment alternative is better for the company than for the individually considered partners.

4. DIVIDENDS

There is the third area of basic decisions in finances. The investors put the stock with the hope to obtain an economic benefit that is moderate in terms of the dividend plus the possible valuation of the share in the market, or the value that can be obtained by accomplishment of the contribution.

When one makes this type of decisions, the executive must be cautious when processing the cash flow as he base to calculate the dividend that can be decreed without affecting the liquidity of the company and to take care of a possible reduces the stock by a bad decision.

In the event of temporary difficulties of capital and with a good perspective of yield, it can be decided on the alternative of dividend in share as a mechanism to preserve its value, protecting the shareholders (about this subject we talk widely in another document).

In summary, we say that the basic objective of the finances is fulfilled by means of the combination of three types of decisions: investment, financing and dividends.

In order to decide it is fundamental that the management studies carefully the external environment (macroeconomic, competition, policies of foreign trade, tributary situation, etc.), and tries to adapt the company to the general conditions for the best benefit. The study of the economic measures is fundamental, measuring the repercussion on the company and its owners, on base of much operative efficiency, because a good financial handling without an efficient activity is not possible, that is to say, if don´t generate value calculated according to the formulate:

$$EVAC_p \text{ (josavere)} = \frac{P_r + I\&D + P_o + Q_u + O}{P + A} - CofC$$

$EVAC_p$: +Corrected and projected EVA
P_r: +Profits of the period
ID: +Investments in investigation and development
P_o: +Investments in able to be capitalized publicity
Q_u: +Qualification
O: +Other able to be capitalized investments properly supported
$C \text{ of } C$: +Cost of capital

One is an indicator very used by the international investors; we write about it later on.

Chapter 4

ANALYSIS OF THE COUNTABLE PRINCIPLES

by josavere

People who are involved in finance and other users of the financial statements Work with companies of all types and interact with all the economic sectors. The best way to choose between several alternatives is the comparison on a homogeneously basis, which is obtained as all the accountants, and therefore the states that they prepare are ruled by the same accounting principles and accounting norms.

In order to inquire about a financial matter one requires a general knowledge of the accounting principles and its effects to be able to interpret the information correctly. The most important principles are:

1. ECONOMIC BODY

The company constitutes a different body from the individuals considered partners. The body concept is different from the "person" concept. The same person can produce financial statements of several individuals or economic bodies.

This principle defines the accounting unit and emphasizes the distinction between the firm and the owners. For that reason, is needed to register the operations to the company and its owners, as equal as with others. The body must be defined in a way in which it can be distinguished from others and able to have exclusive accounting. For practical cases a certificate of constitution and management is required.

Due to this principle, the presentation of a consolidated balance becomes recommendable, especially for economic groups.

2. CONTINUITY

It is assumed that a company has undefined life, except for an express indication on the contrary. Normally, the permanence are expected and not its liquidation.

According to this principle, the value of liquidation does not constitute a criterion for valuation of the assets, with the exception of a special case in which they indicated that the economic entity will not continue working normally due to capital deficiency, accumulated losses, strikes and governmental restrictions, etc.

The generation of monetary founds gains importance, according to which the value of a company or its assets is calculated by its capacity to generate cash flow.

As a consequence of this, it is accepted that the merchandise in process may have some value (depending on a suitable criterion of valuation) even though in a specific stage of production its real value can be zero.

On the other hand, due to this philosophical base the accumulation of expenses expected will appear in the future in order as maintaining the company in an increasing process.

The projection of cash flow constituted at a fundamental accounting statement, replaces the balance ship as bases on the real estimation of the value of an organization, because through it, the risk of falling in to technical insolvency will be calculated. One demands explanatory notes in case of negative tendencies, financial difficulties and other internal or external causes.

3. OBJECTIVITY

The accounting transactions and the financial statements must have plenty of endorsement in reality supported by facts and documents.

For that, by any possible means, verifiable proof must exist objectively. It is possible to be replaced by the criterion of the accountant and the director's body. According to Gredy, the reliability of the accounting data is obtained by means of suitable measures of internal control.

With a little analysis it can be concluded that the accounting measurements have variable degrees of objectivity that depends on the ones that are being moderate and the capacity of those who are doing. Later on, when we analyze the accounting caution, we can see how these principles, in certain way, are somehow contradictory therefore a good criterion of those users of financial statements is demanded.

4. CONSISTENCY OR CONTINUITY

The accounting practices must be applied constantly through time. The application of alternative practices which can give enormously divergent results is avoided.

As in accounting we have several procedures for the same aim (valuation of inventories, calculation of depreciation, recognition of rent, etc.), the selection of a method that better adapts to each particular case and its application year after year is required.

By its application the management manipulation of the results alternatively using different accounting practices is avoided, as could be for example, the estimate of inventories by FIFO (first units in entering, first in leaving) in a period and the following one changing to LIFO (last in entering, first in leaving); this in order to improve the level of profit of the last period.

Of course, in respect to the consistency does not mean that the methods of the accounting, once adopted, can never be changed. If sometime a change is considered advisable more towards another suitable procedure, it is possible, as long as it is complemented with an explanatory note to the financial statements.

5. CAUTIOUSNESS

A profit must be recognized only at the moment of its accomplishment; the lost must be entered with the single expectation, in order to balance a little the not well based optimism.

Another way to interpret it consists of sub valuing the net profits and the accounting capital instead of overvalue them in case of doubt. The principle, in a certain way, is oriented to protect the bankers, the investors and the creditors.

Sometimes an exaggerated application can take away the reality of the information that the financial statements provide, this situation would cause the violation of the objectivity previously commented.

According to Moonitz, the conservative is not more than a warning in order to act in a cautious way considering all the pertinent factors.

In the practice, the preserving doctrine has become the most used tool by the businessman to undervalue the profits and to exaggerate the losses.

With the unrestricted acceptance of this principle, businessmen have found useful resource to reduce profit. The damaged field is the state treasurer because its accounting has been oriented fundamentally with a tributary criterion. Another damaged, without doubt, is the small shareholder who does not have access to the information.

With a batter analysis, the stock-market is clearly explained as the best practical procedure to buy a company, used among other indicators the **Q of Tobin** (the value of share in the market/the intrinsic value).

6. UNIT OF MEASUREMENT

The value of the balance sheet cuts must be expressed in monetary units. The common practice consists of choosing the currency of each country as an instrument to reduce a series of heterogeneous components (machinery, buildings, lands, etc.), to an expression that allows to group them and to compare them easily. This principle makes the accounting nowadays questionable. Since the structure of the accounting discipline began, until some years ago, the accountants assumed that the value of the currency was constant, which is not certain nowadays neither in the United States nor in the European countries and even less in the rest of the world.

7. PERIOD

The economic body must prepare and spread periodic financial statements; the cuts, previously defined in consideration to the cycle of the operations. It must be made a minimum, once a year.

8. PRACTICAL CHARACTERISTICS OF EACH ACTIVITY

The accounting model of each economic body is prepared considering the limitations that in reasonable form impose the customs of each activity, for reasons of social development, economic, technological, geographic, etc.

9. ACCOMPLISHMENT

It forces to recognize the economic facts made solely, that is to say, that it can be verified what they have or will have a benefit or a quantifiable commitment.

10. ASSOCIATION

It indicates that the income of an accounting period must be associated, with the costs and expenses incurred to generate them and to register those incomes simultaneously in the accounts of results.

11. TOTAL REVELATION

It a brief way, the current information due to the financial situation is needed, the experienced changes and their capacity to generate cash flow in the future.

This indicates that in addition to the basic financial statements, the information of managers is integral part of the information as well as the fiscal auditors and the notes of the sheets.

12. ESSENCE ON FORM

The economic facts must not merely be informed according to their essence and legal form.

13. VALUATION OR MEASUREMENT

All the headings of the financial statements must be expressed in monetary terms with subjection to technical norms (updated historical value, present value or of replacement, value of accomplishment or market, discounted present value).

14. MAINTENANCE OF THE EQUITY

It is understood that first of all, the economic body must maintain or recover its equity properly updated in order to reflect the effect of the inflation.

Chapter 5

HANDLING CASH-ELECTRONIC BANK

by josavere

By virtue of almost the entire institutionalization on a worldwide scale of the inflationary phenomenon, the necessity that businessmen learn to coexist with him, such as coffee businessmen learned to produce in the middle of the Roya (coffee leaf rust damage).

Due to the increase of prices, the handling of cash became an important topic. It is actions characterized by the search of mechanisms that allow increase the speed of money circulation; we almost have to think like the people of the countries with galloping inflation: the bill burns the hands, damages the safety boxes and rots the mattresses.

The fastest the currency circulates the less risk of losing the buying capacity. The bank, that traditionally has taken advantage of the unknown of the people in this aspect, has begun to notice the change and has entered with vigor to that market respecting the right of its client to increase the speed of the currency.

The electronic bank represents an excellent advance, but it is not within the reach of all the companies. Subsequently we will refer to it.

1. MECHANISMS FOR THE HANDLING OF THE CASH

- The suitable selection of the bank.
- Concentration in few accounts.
- Special agreements.
- Use floating or retained checks.
- Program the pays.
- Maintain the savings accounts with special negotiations.
- Use the system of nocturnal consignment.
- Open national accounts.
- Establish good relations with its clients.
- Handle the national check.
- Take advantage of the experience.
- To use the computer.
- Use the electronic bank.

A. SUITABLE SELECTION OF THE BANK: the use of a method of points is recommended; some similarly to the implemented one, granted on shares of credit (josavere). It is helpful to use the concept emitted by an examining company of risks. The complexity of the study depends on the account that we hoped to maintain; the banks on the other hand, are competing for the money. Maintains the idea that we are clients and the businesses must be good for both parts as it bases of lasting relations. If the number average to deposit considers discharge, we must begin to study the selection of the bank, using public information.

We happened to study aspects not less important like the range of services, insisting that we needed the most in this particular case. For example, if in regard to the type of business we must mobilize a lot of money in cash, the transport facilities could be a determining factor. The vicinity is another important factor, because it facilitates and it reduces the time of transactions and it diminishes the risk of holdups, robberies, etc., in case that the electronic bank cannot be used.

Previously, a popular saying was very common: "there aren't banks, there are bankers"; meaning, that the relations with the banking executive were the most important. With the electronic bank the worldwide tendency, in the frame of the globalization, will not be worth to be the friend of the manager for the authorization of an overdraft or to obtain a loan. The agencies in the cyberspace, with virtual managers, are the following step in the evolution of the supply of financial services through technology.

In addition to this, it is important to quote that the selected bank must have as much coverage in national and international scope. That is to say, at the moment for making international businesses to be able to count with a bank of confidence with endorsement and guarantor.

B. CONCENTRATION OF MONEY IN FEW BANKS PROPERLY DESCRIBED: a good selection of banks, **diminished the risk** and consequently, the application of the diversification principle is less important. This way it is possible to have few appreciable accounts with the great advantage of being perfectly located by the administration of the bank, facilitating itself any type of operations.

C. SPECIAL AGREEMENTS: it turns out very advisable to enter to negotiate a line of credit even though it is not required, simply to have a factor of tranquility for an unexpected event as it could be an overdraft caused by a check given back by the bank, etc.

Negotiation of remittances, transfer of funds of other cities, acceptance of temporary overdrafts, references etc., constitute example of negotiations that most be celebrated. Great care with the remittances of the towns and groups of judges must be had, to which the banks try to reject, due to the exaggerated slowness on their payments.

D. FLOATING CHECK USE: by diverse circumstances, not always the beneficiaries collect the checks with the diligence that must be, as it explains itself widely in this article. By means of an effective mechanism of information it manages itself to know the availability of this situation and the use of the cash could be done with the necessary care so the insufficiency of funds would not be present at the moment of the presentation of the respective checks.

This type of operations is very common in the weekends and in the holidays.

E. PROGRAMMING OF PAYMENTS: the resulting payment program of the projection of the cash allows to prioritize and to determine dates of payment. A prudent handling agrees not to lose prestige.

It is of **bad taste** the common practice: "payments Friday after 3 p.m." It is elegant, when acquiring commitments to have in mind the dates, using the maximum as possible, and the advantage that can offer the calendar.

As an example, we say that it is not convenient to make a purchase of merchandise to be received on a Holly Wednesday, because we would relinquish four days, unless the good is going to be commercialized or used on that time. In this case, we must program the purchase for the following month. The periods of vacations, strikes, etc., require great care.

F. TO MAINTAIN SAVINGS ACCOUNTS WITH SPECIAL NEGOTIATIONS: in certain cases payments are necessarily gathered by parts based on their quantity; by the impossibility to recover it in a single day. Let's see: let us suppose a treasury with an average of a million daily pesos. The time of Christmas comes near and the payments by legal and extralegal premiums to the personnel are worth a total of ten million. In this case, it corresponds to the man of finances to take the precautions to reunite the cash with periodic savings.

A savings account is used for it and, in addition, it pays monetary correction and interest. With regard to the previous thing it is very important to study the conditions of liquidation of interests as far as date and balances so that the benefit is effective.

Another alternative could be a capitalization policy.

G. TO USE THE NIGHT DEPOSIT: much recommended in businesses where most part of the income appears at night as in the case of entertainment centers in general. This way, the risk of robbery, holdup etc. is reduced, obviously, according to the measures taken with precautions to make the corresponding operations.

H. PARTICULAR AGREEMENTS WITH THE CLIENTS: using good relations, it is possible to be solicited to them that when briefing in t he national unique account they inform immediately so that in the treasury department of the company the availability's of funds are known opportunely, etc. These practices can be motivated through much more dynamic means like Internet through the e-mail (electronic mail), specialize d lines that when calling them, it would be an agile way to info r m the consignment, etc.

I. TO HANDLE THE NATIONAL CHECK: these are checks that can be received or be briefed in any bank office in the country. It represents great security, because it avoids having to travel with great sums of money.

J. TO TAKE ADVANTAGE OF THE EXPERIENCE: the accumulation of experience would be giving great knowledge about the clients, the suppliers and other organizations to which the finance executive is related, which allows him to consider more accurately the cash flow and face difficult situations with good relations, an opportune conversation, a calm temperament, etc.

The reproachable thing is the use of the irresponsible practices and bad taste like the payment of the obligations with check of seats very difficult to make effective in regard to the distance or with errors deliberately committed in its processing, etc.

K. TO USE THE COMPUTER: the extraordinary advance of computer science enormously facilitates the handling of cash.

In effect, the administration of the money depends fundamentally on the exact and opportune information. Nowadays, the manufacturers of computers offer programs of handling of circulating to which the adaptations required for the particular case can be done. Even more, the immense range of new services developed by the bank, are possible by the virtue use of the modern equipment of computation.

L. ELECTRONIC BANK (E.B.): the service of Electronic Bank, is obtained by means of special agreement that operates in a company's computer on line (in real time) connected to a central computer of the bank This method shortens the geographic distances and reduces the time, the scarcest of the resources in the enterprise world. It diminishes costs and it replaces the traditional offices with virtual ones. It is characterized by its exclusivity; direct access by means for different types of uses; own database and permanent technical assistance.

In order to use their services the following minimal requirements of hardware, software and administrative are needed.

a. Requirements of the Hardware:

- Computer with processor 80586 (Pentium) or superior.

- Processing Speed superior to 1.50 MHz or greater if it has multimedia.
- Monitor or screen VGA.
- RAM memory 16 Megabytes, if it has the Windows 95 or superior it must have at least 32 Mb.
- Hard disc with 4 Gigabytes at least, to be able to install several programs.
- Floppy Disk drives 3,5 inches of Discharge.
- Modem, preferably external and compatible.
- Hayes (for the modem) with minimum speed of 2400 megahertz, installed in an available serial port.
- Asynchronous cards of communications with exit RS232.
- Standard telephone line of direct access or fiber optical for connection.

b. Requirements of Software:

- To have installed Windows 95 or superior (Windows 95 extra or 98).
- 10 Megabytes available in Hard Disk to install the program.
- Install some navigator for Internet (Explorer or Netscape).
- Install a program for handling the electronic mail.
- Install some applications that will help maintain the control on the banking accounts.
- Install Antiviral program with periodic updates.
- Optionally it would be possible to have in the PC, a compressor of programs to compress copies of the transactions, so that it does not occupy greater space in the disc.

c. Administrative Requirements:

- Decide the type of computers to buy or to rent.
- To define which person are going to have a shared work.
- Decide how many hours in the day the connection with Internet will be on.
- To determine how many transactions will be made daily or monthly so a decision on which Internet supplier will be affiliated can be made.
- To select the people who are going to be dedicated to record the banking transactions.
- To well establish the policy on copy support, indicating the responsible people.

The Electronic Bank is located in the intersection of three elements that have evolved in joint form and parallel: on one hand, hardware and software, by the other, telecommunications, and finally the financial services; the strongest revolution had taken place in the term of the telecommunications and in some atmospheres, related to the technology which make this a reality.

In the cyber-society there are no checks, neither savings checkbooks, nor forms of credit request, nor receipts of payment; what it does have is millions of transactions through the network. The success will depend on the capacity of the financial organization to supply its products in an efficient and effective way. With simple operations that can be of massive use because the high investments in technology get to be profitable on the base of a high number of clients and transactions.

The electronic bank allows transactions to be made in a reliable way by the use of three types of password (keys): operative, of authorization and card. It offers confidentiality because the data are sent together and compressed avoiding that information can be infiltrated. When compressing, it also diminishes the transmissions cost.

By the agility and comfort that offers, is ideal to make financial transactions from the office or the home; it reduces the inherent risks of using messengers and handling cash; it diminishes the costs of stationery and their elaboration.

In the middle of so many advantages it offers a very serious problem: the risk of information. If this one is lost by any circumstance it destroys the reliability of the system. Also, the intersection of the line when a transaction is made, with which is possible to do withdrawals simulating an entity.

A risk that is taken is one person in the handling of the tool that gives possibility to detect the password; the person enters the login and without verifying that it does not have the error message the password is copied, being known by whoever is monitoring the movements.

It is necessary that all the financial organizations and most of the automatic accountant, received the certificate of quality ISO 9002 This act of transcendental importance that will serve as base for an accelerated development of the Electronic Bank by the confidence that instills the users and by the application in specialized transactions of titles values and general, in every type of businesses that are made in the Stock markets and the electronic commerce.

2. GENERAL SCHEME ACTION / PARTITION OF THE ELECTRONIC BANK

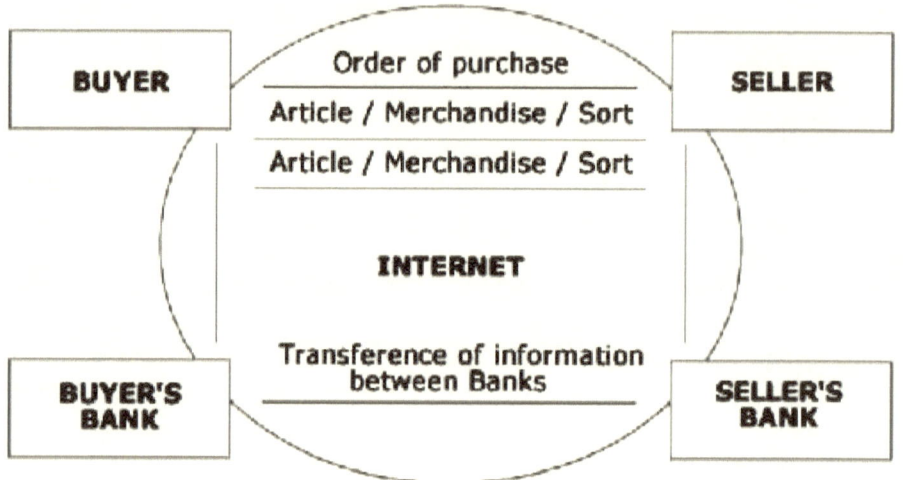

Absolutely all the services have a tariff that serves as base to calculate the volume of operations that justify such important development, in which the most important are:

a. Integral portfolio or scoring: it does the work of factoring.

b. Call Center: communication with no need to identify itself because the mechanism does it directly, offers consultations, payments and transfers. The operations by this mean are more economic than in the network agencies. It allows to offer services in remote places and to make operations 24 hours a day, 7 days a week.

c. Self in Express: it allows making all the operations from the address including cash transport and the enterprise exchange installed terminals in each company.

d. Interbank: connection with Internet to execute all types of transactions by electronic mail.

e. Electronic commerce: without geographic or national borders facilitating negotiations with any place of the world, shortening the delivery problems

f. Movable terminals: terminals that can go to the place where the client is and with the apparatus consult the balance make payments and open up loans.

In summary, we can say that the handling of cash requires so much care as any other asset and, why not say it, more than all of them because the money is lost easily in regard to the moral deterioration, declared mainly in thefts, holdups, robberies, etc.

Aside from the specific cares related to the proper handling, which is only entrusted to people of proven moral solvency, a great dominion of the techniques enumerated here are required. And any other one can be named to avoid the acquisitive power or the reduction of the yield by excess of liquidity.

With regard to the physical cares of the cash, they must be carried far safety measure, because it is the most liquid of the assets or goods of a society and, in addition, the fraud effect, self-loans, robberies, holdups, would diminish the liquidity situation directly.

Mechanisms for the physical care, the following ones must be mentioned, and like it is logical, others that can be contributed with the security which never will exceed:

A. CUSTODY: the cares that are due to implant in the referring thing to the cash, must begin from the own moment in which it is collected, and does not end with the deposit in the bank but with its verification. It must be done by a person who reunites the conditions of honorably and responsibility, in addition to a handling policy and keep it in a safety box preferably with two passwords, one handled by the person in charge (treasurer or accountant) and the other by a representative of reviser.

B. PERIODIC ARCHING: practicing unexpected periodic arching ; must take place at the first hour of the day) allows us to assure us if the received cash that are kept and consigned in the same form in which they were received. Because it happens that in some cases appear loses or there are checks cashing without some authorization, or by some cause not all the received are deposited (exception of post dew checks), situations that come to the light by means of the arching of cash box.

C. VERIFICATION OF BALANCES: it is advisable, periodic confirmation with the banks and corporations of the balances to a determined date, with the purpose of CROSSING, with the auxiliary registries of box and banks.

D. BANKING CONCILIATION: it is required to opportunely conciliate the current accounts and of savings, since in some cases notes appeared debit to the account; sometimes deposit errors appear and if they are not found out quickly, can cause a overdraft in the account. An opportune investigation allows to know clearly the situation and to take the remedial actions.

E. CONFIRMATION OF DESERVING BALANCES: the practices of one good audit demands that at least once a year the balances of the suppliers and creditors of the company are confirmed, with the purpose of not paying more liabilities and not receiving less than what corresponds.

F. TRANSPORT: when the volume of cash that is handled demands the hiring of a transporter of values, it does not have to be doubted in making it so that the risk of holdup is diminished such as robbery or loss.

G. GUARANTEES AND INSURANCES: it is necessary that all the civil employees who in some way or another handle cash present their policies of handling and fulfillment. At the moment, it is essential to take all kind of precautions; and among them to take the insurance from the case, with the purpose of diminishing the risk.

H. ALLOCATION OF FUNCTIONS: for the specific case of the cash it is advisable to avoid that employee makes the reception functions, deposit and payments in chain. He always must have interruptions that facilitate the internal control, (an employee controls another one).

I. APPROVAL OF PAYMENTS: this mechanism being the last one is not less important, on the contrary, the good administration of the cash demands the immediate identification of the responsible civil employee as far as amounts, date, place, etc.

The acceptance of this responsibility must be demonstrated in the document of payment or it's on default in the supports, by means of code, initial, name, etc.

CHAPTER 6

ADMINISTRATION OF PORTFOLIO

by josavere

INTRODUCTION

Dr Carlos Restrepo D. my grand teacher, defined the portfolio as the **"own bank"**. In effect, within the conception of an industrial business, the operative cycle begins with a design and the purchase of raw materials; continuing with the productive process, payment of manual labor and other expenses and, he finishes with the sale and the collection of portfolio. Logically, every day cycles begin and end. The normal situation in business is that the current assets must be superior to the current liabilities. If the financial structure of a business is rare, but in some special cases, the current assets must be minor to the current liabilities. Maintaining the inventories within the limits when defining the proportion of assets, it is expected that the portfolio produces resources sufficient to take care of the obligations of short term. Nevertheless, in most of the cases the portfolio rather than the bank constitutes **a true problem**. Often cases of companies occur that in spite of presenting good indicators of liquidity, they face serious difficulties of circulating and permanently they must resort to the market of money in search of huge expensive solutions.

In order to make the decision to sell on credit, an evaluation must be made in economic terms, comparing additional profit sales a waited for with the **rate of cut** of the company and an overhaul of the direct and indirect costs; of course, the financial standing consulted to decide if the company has the work capital necessary to maintain the operation that generates the sales on credit.

In general terms, the sale on credit is easier than the sales on cash, so desirable in finance. But the conditions of the market, the economic characteristics of the competition and conditions in some cases, force most of the companies to sell on credit. The caution, accounting basic rule, recommends not to recognize the sale until is not a reality. In administrative language, in the case of sales we can say that we don't accept it as such until the proper collection. In this order of ideas, we do not have to be satisfied placing numbers with sales, nor with making profits in books; these are due to be noticed in the cash flow, which depends in good proportion, on the collections of portfolio.

1. HOW TO SELECT A CLIENT

Let's begin to observe a credit request, because this constitutes the fundamental tool to know the person or organization with whom we are going to establish relationship. Let's remember that while greater the selection effort, which has to do with the entailment although at first it implies too much investment, in the long run it widely will be compensated with the smaller effort of collection from delays in payments and with the losers by noncollectable portfolio. On the contrary, a selection to the light one leads to greater losses from delays and nonpayment.

Credit Application

Applicant Information

Name:			
Date of birth:	SSN:		Phone:
Current address:			
City:	State:		ZIP Code:
Own Rent (Please circle)	Monthly payment or rent:		How long?
Previous address:			
City:	State:		ZIP Code:
Owned Rented (Please circle)	Monthly payment or rent:		How long?

Employment Information

Current employer:			
Employer address:			How long?
Phone:	E-mail:		Fax:
City:	State:		ZIP Code:
Position:	Hourly Salary (Please circle)		Annual income:
Previous employer:			
Address:			How long?
Phone:	E-mail:		Fax:
City:	State:		ZIP Code:
Position:	Hourly Salary (Please circle)		Annual income:
Name of a relative not residing with you:			
Address:			Phone:
City:	State:		ZIP Code:

Credit Application for a Business Account

Business Contact Information

Title:			
Company name:			
Phone:	Fax:		E-mail:
Registered company address:			
City:		State:	ZIP Code:
Date business commenced:			
Sole proprietorship:	Partnership:	Corporation:	Other:

Business and Credit Information

Primary business address:			
City:		State:	ZIP Code:
How long at current address?			
Telephone:	Fax:	E-mail:	
Bank name:			
Bank address:		Phone:	
City:		State:	ZIP Code:
Type of account	Account number		
Savings			

Commercial Credit Application

| TO | Name / Address / City/State/Zip / Credit Mgr / Phone | | FROM | Name / Address / City/State/Zip / E-Mail / Phone |

Business Type: ☐ Sole Proprietor ☐ Partnership ☐ Corporation: State _____
How long in business: _____   D&B Number: _____

Names/Addresses of Individuals or Partners -or- Name/Title/Phone Number of Corporate Officers

Name of Person to Contact Regarding Purchase Orders and Invoices, Title, Address, and Phone

Bank Reference   Account Number, Contact, Title, and Phone Number

Trade References: Company Name, Address, Contact and Title, and Phone Number

The above information is submitted for the sole purpose of opening an account and I hereby certify the information to be true.

SIGNED _____
TITLE _____
DATE _____

The collection expectation basically depends on a good selection of credit; generally, the wide range of organizations and people ask for it. The decision is difficult by itself, among other things, by the pressure of the salesmen of the company and because it implies to find a balance between risk and the yield, because in the measurement that grants the credit or the terms that are extended are frozen cash in accounts to receive and it endangers the capacity to cover liabilities.

The greater difficulty appears in the evaluation of the portfolio management because an interval exists of generally enough time between the decision of granting the credit and the moment that we accept the impossibility to receive the account.

Briefly, an organization realizes that his Head of Credit did his work badly when the problem is already created, and hardly detects deficiencies in the management with the opportunity that is required.

In most cases, the decision of the credit is very subjective and delicate. In order to avoid this difficulty the companies must design a model that allows them, whenever is possible, "to objectivity" the decision.

A good system could be to establish a Manual of Credits, according to point previously established. The Manual will say: if it has so many points, its line of credit will be of so many dollars complemented with software that allows in addition to the qualitative quantitative and analysis the corresponding one.

2. ANALYSIS ELEMENTS

a. IDENTIFICATION OF THE CLIENT: certificate of existence and legal representation, providing evidence on the existence of the company, fulfillment of legal commitments, manages mental capacity to assume commitments, etc.

b. THE FINANCIAL STATEMENT OF THE APPLICANT: for the case one is due to mainly makes emphasis in the aspects of liquidity and indebtedness and, in the value generation.

The analysis must be made very carefully, maintain the limitations of the financial statements and thinking about a commercial sense. It does not matter that a company becomes broke, thus we have guaranteed the debt. It is ideal to work with projected financial statements, properly sustained; centering the analysis in the state of cash flow, since while the cash projection is positive it eases the fulfillment of the obligations.

c. REFERENCES: commonly one asks for concerning references. Usually this one present its friends, who in the great majority of the cases, recommend him very well. Who is going to present/display as informant to a person or organization with which there was some problem? This type of information is to be gathered; it must be cross examined with a credit information center.

It is essential that all the organizations that grant credits be link end to another "Great Organization", that would be the possessor one of all the commercial information and the behavior of the users of the credit.

That organization would be the possessor one of all the information and therefore it will be in capacity to objectively inform to any person or organization who asks for a credit.

In addition it would have to exist, quite a difficult thing, a gentleman's pact, in order to accept religiously the received information and to block the bad creditors. This mechanism is oriented to protect the company that specially grants credits, because the law by its slowness protects widely from the bad creditors, to the corrupt ones.

d. GUARANTEES: every operation of credit involves a risk factor. A good form to reduce it consists on asking for guarantees to the beneficiary who must be soon to grant them to the commitment proportionally. It is said commonly, "To a good creditor the debts won't hurt him".

The guarantee must have a value of accomplishment sufficient to totally cover the legal debt, interests and other expenses that the collection by channel implies.

The best one of all is the fiduciary, because it makes agile transactions and the real estate constitutes a "lasting currency" in inflationary economies, safe in conditions of financial crises or of another order. In addition they can be mortgaging, banking, negotiable titles values whose fulfillment is due to agree in the place where the company that grants the credit operates anticipating, a problem of judicial collection, which they serve as well to acquire money in financial organizations by means of the mechanism of discount.

e. OTHERS: (It is recommended to consult legal aspects: concordats, bankruptcy and liquidations.) although it seems obvious and elementary that they are good to stress the following aspects:

— To maintain the accounts very clear: the client must receive a bank statement where the positions and the causes are explained to him clearly.
— To try good relationships with the client: one is due to know the basic information of the clients.

Once identified the client it helps to focus the efforts with the purpose of concentrating the efforts in the most representative buyers. The differentiation serves to decide the suitable strategy of collection. The conservation of the clients through telephone calls, personal visits, or by more advanced channels as the electronic mail.

— To define a payment application order: the first interests if they appear and soon the invoices in victory order.
— The client must sign the invoice on arrival of the merchandise and the interests from delayed payment are due in agreement with the

invoice.—The commissions for salary to salesmen due to be distributed, starting off when selling and complement when receiving the cash.

3. FINANCIAL ASPECTS

In financial terms, to sell on credit is equivalent to reduce prices. This varies based on the cost of capital and the term; the calculation has been eased considerably by the technological advances.

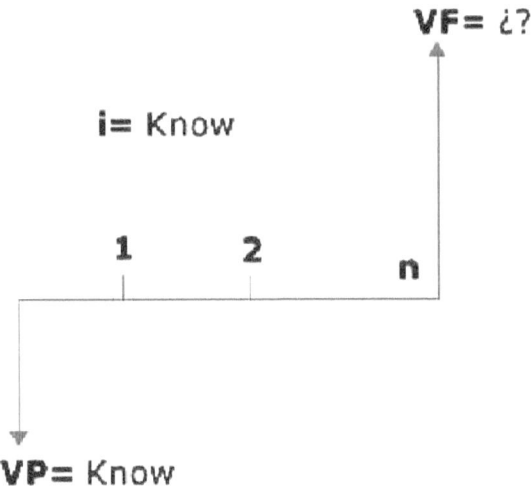

One has to calculate the present value of a future income (price) discounted at an interest rate in an equal period. A company that sell in terminus of four months, sells monetary units at 88 8487%, if we assumed an interest rate of 3%.

VP =? (Unknown)

$$\begin{aligned} VF: & \quad +100 \\ \text{(Monthly) } i: & \quad +3\% \\ n: & \quad +4 \text{ months} \\ P: & \quad +.888487 \end{aligned}$$

This analysis is important when it is going to make the decision to fix sale prices, for to calculate or the yield of products, or the **margin of contribution**.

If the payment is by equivalent fees, the same calculation can be done. In this case it is to calculate given P a R.

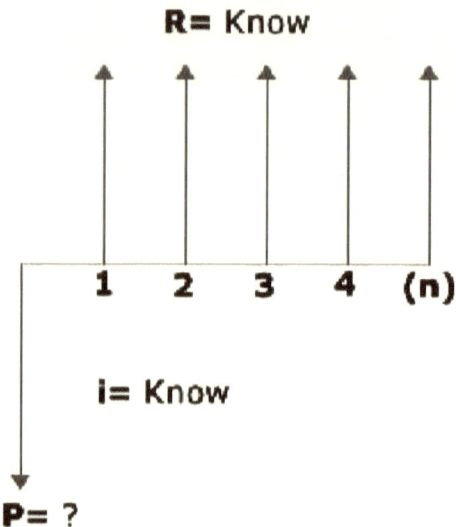

Once the decision is made of the term to grant, the efforts are due to direct to treat of which the portfolio recovers before the decided moment or if it is possible. How?

A. DISCOUNTS BY PROMPT PAYMENT: in the monetary market a permanent dispute by the money appears. For the governors the easier measures to fight inflation are the monetary ones and therefore they go for them, permanently restricting the circulating (cash) in greater or smaller degree, depending on the general situation.

The company must enter to compete with aggressiveness in that market, offering attractive discounts, so the best investment for the client is to cancel before the victory. Among other things, intermediaries are not needed; it does not imply retention at the source, nor specialist's studies. In general, the decision to" invest" is due to present the easier possible for the clients; it must be eliminated per days to avoid concentration of payments in the deadline and must be applied in as strict form as the circumstances allow it.

B. INTERESTS FROM DELAYED PAYMENTS: the interests from delayed payment must have the punitive character and therefore to be higher than the interest rate that appears in the market. Of this form it is avoided that the clients finance with the supplier, system used nowadays, due to its inexpensiveness, in addition it does not require study of credit nor guarantees, nor approvals of meetings and other papers for the loans in financial organizations.

For the effect the consultation of legal aspects is recommended in order to avoid difficulties that can arise by violations that can end in damage to the company that grants the credit.

C. RECONSTRUCTION OR REFINANCING OF THE CREDIT: in some cases the reconstruction of the debt is recommendable, for which it asks for an indebted document update, with the purpose of signing documentation as if it were a new credit; conditioned to pay the first interests from delayed payment sooner, soon the current interests and later the remaining of the debt.

4. WITH FINANCIAL INTERMEDIARIES

A. FACTORING: a financial-administrative alternative that allows yielding portfolio to be overcome and to obtain in return financial advance payments without increasing the indebtedness, easing an adapted handling of the cash flow. Given the importance of this subject we will talk about it in another charter.

B. OTHERS: agreements as securitization, outsourcing can be carried out to allow to contract with the third activity of portfolio administration and contribute to improve the cash flow.

Finally, is important to remember that while the more efficiency is obtained in the study of credits, greater will be the probability of collecting without delays, reason why is recommended to take good care of this kind of decisions framing them in policies defined clearly by the top management, which must be of strict compliance by the group of civil employees with whom they have to do, in the sales and collecting departments.

When notice deviations of the established norms must act with much firmness on the part of the top management. The accumulation of experiences on the behavior of the clients, the geographic zones, the times of the year, etc. will serve as base to perfect more the mechanism of portfolio administration. Also it must be to remember that the most valuable assets of a company are: the human resource, the information, the knowledge and the liquidity.

Chapter 7

HOW TO DEFINE THE GRANTING OF CREDIT
(method of josavere)

by josavere

Accepting that to grant credit is a difficult decision, we take care to do it the most objective possible way in order to facility practice a preventive audit.

The granting of credit is very risky, because the management becomes aware from which this one has been badly granted when the problem is already created. Hardly, in the first stage (while the credit has not been overcome), one knows that a portfolio director is wrongly selected to the clients granting credits in a deficient form.

The great advantage of the system of points to grant credits consists in the possibility that offers to objectivity the decision. Who guarantees that a portfolio director does not grant credits in bad faith and for personal benefits? That does it simply applies to bad criterion?

If the company fixes parameters for granting credit is easy to request justification for one decision. The method, becomes a support and it guarantees a of pattern uniforms of measurement and consistent even though change the employees.

With the object of making comparisons, the quantitative methods are very practice and first of all, they allow us to obtain defined results clearly.

The establishment of a manual of credits with points constitutes a measurement pattern that helps us to compare a natural or legal person with another one and to decide how much credit we can grant objectivity.

The technique consists on designing a manual with which a number of points that are assigned, base on a scale previously established that quantifies the different factors.

1. VARIABLES TO CONSIDER

We selected characteristics that are quaintly by degrees; these must be common to all the potential clients and must facility the establishment differences among them.

Each company or business will design its own manual considering the specific characteristics of its clients, the conditions of the competition and their general direction towards the assumption of risk.

In the case of natural people the following variables will be used among others:

2. NATURAL PEOPLE

A. UNEMPLOYMENT: generally, a person who has a category tries to take care of her/his image. In addition, the job guarantees periodic income.

B. PERIODIC INCOME: the greater the wage level and income of diverse kind, the greater the capacity to meet the payments.

C. IT CALLS TO ACCOUNT: who ever have real state has ties to a city, and in general principle, he tends to remain in it.

D. TELEPHONE, FAX OR ELECTRONIC MAIL (E-MAIL): it facility enormously speeds up the communication for all the related effects.

E. YEARS IN THE LAST USE: it is a symptom of stability in the job. It is especially useful when one of them is consumption credit.

F. AGE: a certain relationship between the age of a person and its life expectancy, its interest in maintaining good reputation and its attitude towards the fulfillment of commitments.

G. CIVIL STATE: normally the unmarried ones have fewer commitments than the married ones; but they also tend to be more disordered in their expenditures.

H. PATRIMONIAL ENDORSEMENT: assets of the applicant that in breach of contract circumstances they could enter endorsing the debt.

I. INDEBTEDNESS LEVEL: the knowledge of the effective debts helps to have one more and more reasonable base about its credit behavior and to define its potential for indebtedness.

3. COMPANIES

A. TYPE OF SOCIETY: independent of other considerations, the joint-stock companies offer fewer risks than limited and these also less than the collective ones. This factor can be joined up with the years of operation of the society.

B. GRANTED GUARANTEE: the guarantee that has less risk is the letter of credit in addition to being very liquid being indispensable to its victory in immediate form. In contrary the bills of exchange do not offer almost any guarantee.

C. FINANCIAL SITUATION: a careful study of the financial statements of a company, specially the cash flow, allows predicting, with a certain degree of certainty its capacity of payment among others, it is possible to be analyzed: the liquidity, indebtedness, operative cycle and proportion of fixed assets on the total assets cover and yield. In this aspect it is important to remember that the result cannot be taken literally from an index it, is necessary that the analysis be made altogether; considering the limitations of the financial analysis and the alternatives to improve it.

D. TIME OF COMMERCIAL ENTAILMENT: the historical record on the commercial relationships allows predicting the behavior of the clients, taking advantage of the experience.

E. GEOGRAPHIC LOCATION: in the big urban centers collection is speed up because they visit several clients taking advantage of the time. In addition, the airlines and telephone and other services offer great advantages. An errand in New York is very different from another one in Denver.

F. IMAGE: this one is detected through the looks of the business, the acceptance of credit cards, its location in the sector of the city, trajectory of the company, time of activity and its acceptance in society.

G. ECONOMIC SECTOR: because it eases the analysis in the measurement in which it allows comparisons according to the general conditions of the economy and the sector individually.

4. ASSIGN A WEIGHT TO THE FACTORS

Once selected the factors to be considered, we come to its apprising. For it, the constitution of a committee of heterogeneous nature is recommended and in which they must take part, people from an independent criterion; each one will emit its own judgment about the relative weight of each one of the factors, for example, two members of a committee will be able to distribute the score in the following form:

Factors	A (%)	B (%)
1. Type of society	15	12
2. Granted guarantee	20	20
3. Financial situation	25	20
4. Time of commercial relationships	10	8
5. Geographic location	10	20
6. Image	10	10
7. Economic sector	10	10

Later, a confrontation appear of the emitted judgments and by means of application of the statistic it will arrive at an appraisal that will be used for make the manual. When differences are very ample appear, continuing with a process of discussion and analysis that allows to join the members or, to obtain greater objectivity. Example:

Factors	Examining					Weighed qualification	Statistical measurement
	A	B	C	D	E		
1. Type of society	25	20	30	25	25	25	Mode
2. Granted guarantee	20	30	30	25	20	25	Mean
3. Financial situation	15	20	15	15	15	15	Mode
4. Time of commercial relationships	5	5	10	5	5	10	Mode
5. Geographic location	5	5	5	10	5	15	Mean
6. Image	10	15	5	10	15	10	Mean
7. Economic sector	30	20	25	30	10	15	Mean

Once it is obtained the appraisal of factors we continue to the corresponding subdivision. With a base of 100 adapted to maximum credit, we deduce the variation rank which each factor will have. For example, the largest score that can be granted to a company according to the type of society will be 25 points. Obviously the minimum would be zero.

We continued subdividing each of the factors in the different variables that can be presented/displayed in it and we assigned the corresponding score according to the hierarchical structuring that it becomes. For example:

Hierarchical structuring

Grade	Explanation	Points
1	Joint-stock company	Up to 10
2	Limited Society	Up to 9
3	Limited partnership by shares	Up to 8
4	Simple limited partnership	Up to 7
5	Collective Society	Up to 6
6	Impersonal Company	Up to 6
7	Official Company Even	Up to 2

Once the manual is drafted, we continued with the processing of the of fees chart. For it, we entered to study the statistics of the company as far as the quota of credit of the clients who are effective. Thus we calculated fitted maximum that the company has granted.

This is equivalent to the Maximum purchase that hopes in the event that the clients continue themselves tolerating in the same form.

Complemented this information with the criterion of the executives of sales, that among other considerations, will try to avoid the concentration in one client(s) and, anticipating the possible increase of prices in the period for which one is going away to apply the manual, it is defined fitted maximum that the company decides to grant to each one of them.

A potential buyer that accumulates 100 points by means of the sum of invoices, assigned in agreement with its specific location in each one they, will obtain fitted maximum, which is practically theoretical, because hardly will be somebody that describes very optimally in all the factors.

Once fitted maximum with the scale of points, we obtain the rate by each one. Example:

It fitted maximum: 10 million weights

Maximum points: 100

r = 10'000.000 / 100 = $100.000 by each point

No. Points	It fitted of Credit ($)
1	100.000
2	200.000
"	"
"	"
"	"
10	10.000.000

5. GENERAL CONSIDERATIONS

a. The manual must be considered as a guide. In cases of doubt, is necessary *the good criterion of the executives. Like general rule, the cups* will leave by means of the routine application the manual; special cases require considerations of qualitative type.

b. The quotas of credit due to be reviewing periodically in agreement with the change that each client presents and that appear in the policies of the company as the experience is accumulated. In addition, general adjustment will become when they vary prices.

c. The introduction of the technique, like almost all the innovations, will present initial difficulties in its application. In the measurement that allows to the handling of situations and its respective feedback it, the pertinent adjustments will become until obtaining a high degree of reliability.

d. It is a serious error, to copy a manual. Each company must study its particular case and design its own model.

e. It is advisable that audits the application of the manual and applied the experience in the improvement.

f. It is understood that requirements are due to fix minimum to reunite by all the clients to be able to be object of the study. These requirements do not give points.

g. For have good consultant's office before signing any document is important, be because legally, all the financial organizations are authorized to receive sanctions by slow payments. Of not being briefed in the document any collection cannot take place.

h. Among others we can enumerate:

- Transaction of form to ask for credit.
- Sales contract acceptance and fulfillment on credit, in case that it exists.
- Presentation of financial statements.
- Good references, provided preferably by specialized organizations.

Example of a Manual

I. Pond ration of the Committee

Factors	Examining					Weighed qualification	Statistical measurement
	A	B	C	D	E		
1. Type of society	10	3	5	5	10	7	Mean
2. Granted guarantee	24	24	24	30	24	24	Mode
3. Financial situation	30	33	28	25	30	30	Mean
4. Time of commercial relationships	5	5	5	5	5	5	Mode
5. Geographic location	5	4	5	5	5	5	Mode
6. Image	10	11	7	5	5	8	Mean
7. References	10	6	5	5	5	5	Mode
8. Economic sector	5	14	8	20	16	16	Mean

I. Pond ration of Factors

A. TYPE OF SOCIETY: maximum score 7

1. Joint-stock company	7
2. Society in C. x actions	6
3. Society in simple C.	6
4. Limited society	5
5. Impersonal Society	4
6. Without profit spirit	4
7. Society in fact	3
8. Natural Person	1

B. GUARANTEE: maximum score 24

1.	Fiduciary guarantee	24
2.	Letter of credit	18
3.	Check	15
4.	Promissory note	10
5.	Letter of change	5

C. FINANCIAL SITUATION: maximum score 30

1.	Liquidity	12
2.	Indebtedness	8
3.	Activity	5
4.	Yield	5

Note: The score is assigned with base in the corresponding indicators *(to see financial analysis)*.

D. TIME OF COMMERCIAL ENTAILMENT: maximum score 5

1.	More than 3 years	5
2.	Between 2 and 3 years	2
3.	Between 1 year and less than 2 years	3
4.	Less of a year	0

E. GEOGRAPHIC LOCATION: maximum score 5

1.	Metropolitan	5
2.	Zone A	4
3.	Zone B	3
4.	Others	1

F. IMAGE: maximum score 8

1.	Presentation	3
2.	Publicity	2
3.	Credit cards	1
4.	Systematized Information	1
5.	License of Operation	1

G. REFERENCES: maximum score 5

1.	Well referenced	2
2.	Without given back checks	2
3.	Active clients	1

H. ECONOMIC SECTOR: Maximum score 16

1.	Mining	16
2.	Services	14
3.	Telecommunications	12
4.	Farming	11
5.	Commercial	9
6.	Foods	8
7.	Plastics	6
8.	Metal mechanic	6
9.	Automotive	5
10.	Footwear	5
11.	Textile	2
12.	Construction	2

6. PROCESSING OF THE QUOTAS TABLE

For our case it was possible maximum to grant is of dollars 10,000,000, the amount of weights, which is equivalent to 10,000 dollars by point.

r = $ 10.000.000 / 10 = $ 100.000

TABLE OF VALUES BY POINTS

Punts	Valor	Punts	Valor	Punts	Valor	Punts	Valor
100	10.000.000	71	7.100.000	42	4.200.000	13	1.300.000
99	9.900.000	70	7.000.000	41	4.100.000	12	1.200.000
98	9.800.000	69	6.900.000	40	4.000.000	11	1.100.000
97	9.700.000	68	6.800.000	39	3.900.000	10	1.000.000
96	9.600.000	67	6.700.000	38	3.800.000	9	900.000
95	9.500.000	66	6.600.000	37	3.700.000	8	800.000
94	9.400.000	65	6.500.000	36	3.600.000	7	700.000
93	9.300.000	64	6.400.000	35	3.500.000	6	600.000
92	9.200.000	63	6.300.000	34	3.400.000	5	500.000
91	9.100.000	62	6.200.000	33	3.300.000	4	400.000
90	9.000.000	61	6.100.000	32	3.200.000	3	300.000
89	8.900.000	60	6.000.000	31	3.100.000	2	200.000
88	8.800.000	59	5.900.000	30	3.000.000	1	100.000
87	8.700.000	58	5.800.000	29	2.900.000		
86	8.600.000	57	5.700.000	28	2.800.000		
85	8.500.000	56	5.600.000	27	2.700.000		
84	8.400.000	55	5.500.000	26	2.600.000		
83	8.300.000	54	5.400.000	25	2.500.000		
82	8.200.000	53	5.300.000	24	2.400.000		
81	8.100.000	52	5.200.000	23	2.300.000		
80	8.000.000	51	5.100.000	22	2.200.000		
79	7.900.000	50	5.000.000	21	2.100.000		
78	7.800.000	49	4.900.000	20	2.000.000		
77	7.700.000	48	4.800.000	19	1.900.000		
76	7.600.000	47	4.700.000	18	1.800.000		
75	7.500.000	46	4.600.000	17	1.700.000		
74	7.400.000	45	4.500.000	16	1.600.000		
73	7.300.000	44	4.400.000	15	1.500.000		
72	7.200.000	43	4.300.000	14	1.400.000		

Chapter 8

PRACTICAL ASPECTS OF THE HANDLING OF INVENTORIES

by josavere

The theoreticians in this matter present a model to minimize the cost of handling of inventories and to calculate the optimal order that only has application in exceptional cases.

$$Q = \sqrt{\frac{2 V C_p}{K C}}$$

- Q: amount of order (large economic batch)
- V: annual sales
- C: cost per unit
- Cp: cost of placing an order
- K: cost of unit cost maintenance of the inventory, as a % of total of the

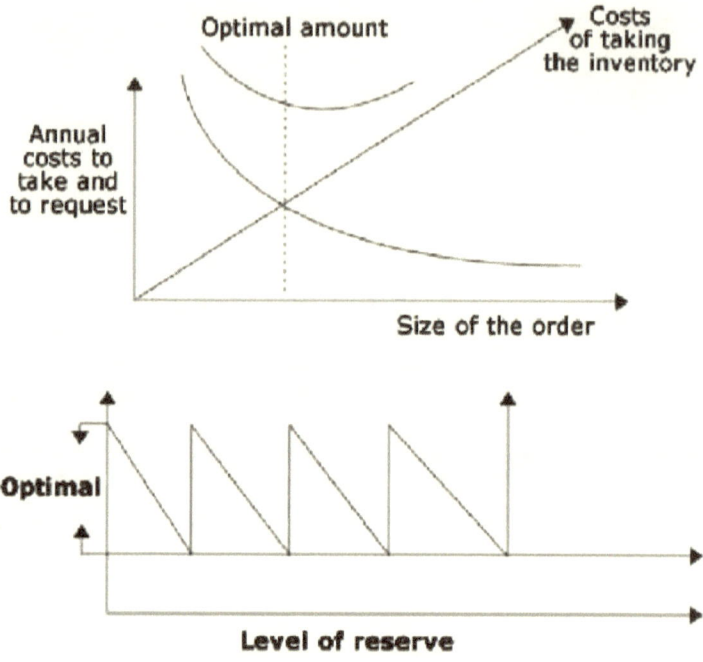

The model bases the calculation on the cost of a unit and the value of placing an order.

In storage, even though it is contracted with third parties, two possibilities exist: the first, that the warehouses are their own, in which case the industrialist incur in the cost of opportunity plus the maintenance costs or renting of the warehouse.

The heading acquires characteristics of fixed and consequently it loses his variability in relation to the units that are stored. The same thing happens to the value of processing an order. The theoreticians speak of the cost of the paper work plus the time it takes to process the order. Who can measure the cost of ink when it is placing an order? How much cost the paper?

In the immense majority of the cases, the order is studied in different center from which indeed it is placed, with the common characteristic that both, employees or executives have fixed assignments and, the time of processing an order is not measurable, with the methods developed by Industrial Engineering.

In addition to the previous considerations, the model assumes requirements that do not appear commonly:

- The supplier is permanently expecting to dispatch immediately.
- The products are homogeneous.
- The production and demands are constant.
- Restrictions in when it do not exist to conditions of suppliers.
- The qualitative aspects do not influence it for anything. It is assumed that the economy is stable.

And the model assumed, in the case of imported merchandise, that the governmental organizations are very diligent to transact the import licenses; that in the ports there are very honest and efficient people working; that the trucks are always available a waiting to be unloaded etc.

The previous considerations are sufficiently explicit to illustrate the initial affirmation. The handling of inventories is not a problem which can be solved by means of a mathematical formula, although the generally used indicators contribute to an efficient administration.

A measurement very used in financial analyses is the rotation of inventories to measure the efficiency in the administration of these assets, which are calculated according to the function:

$$Ir = \frac{CMV}{(Ii + If)/2} = times$$

Ir: rotation of inventories
CMV: cost of the merchandise sold
Ii: initial inventory
If: final inventory

Previous function: $Ir = CMV / [(Ii + If)/2] = times$.

In addition to the limitations of the financial analysis, is important to bring the famous phrase:" statistical is the science that if you have eaten a chicken and I have not eaten anything, in average each one would have eaten half a chicken."

According to the law of the big numbers, the series of data tend to concentrate around a value or measurement of central tendency that is the measurement of rotation of inventories.

Using a frequent distribution of short periods (months) and used the suitable measurement (the fashion, medium or the average arithmetic) the problem is that ignoring the dispersion measures. It is very probable that in the inventories we find a series of products of highest rotation; some of average rotation and others of slow rotation.

The law of Paretto talks about efforts for 20% to handle 80% of products and vice verse. What at first look like sight "genius" advice, is that products are left a side and concentrate the activities in others. This common affirmation, obeys to the purely mathematical analysis, the merely cold calculation.

The great superiority of men over machines is exactly in the qualitative analysis or of criterion, what it is not possible to be exposed numerically. It corresponds to the management calculate indices for similar groups looking for the indicator that provides information to us adapted for an efficient handling.

I. WHAT TO DO?

Is good complementing the mathematical models with the method of trial and error. We go step by step:

A. INDUSTRIAL COMPANIES: in this sector it is necessary to analyze four types of inventories: raw materials, finished products, in process and spare parts.

a. Finished product: if the company properly prepares a plan of value generation, it will be able to determine for the different times of the year the levels of finished product inventory, in accordance with the estimation of the demand. Arithmetically it will be:

$$If = Ii + Pp - Ve$$

If: final inventory (budgeted)
Ii: initial inventory
Pp: programmed production
Ve: projected sales

The periodic control of the results with the budgets will be indicating if they are due to make greater or smaller number of units in each type, depending on the success that has been obtained when projecting the sales.

The analysis of the characteristics of the product is very recommendable (In case they are perishable, volatile, etc.) and the relations with the suppliers.

That way we have an element of control and analysis. The periodic revision obeys to a master plan that contemplates the projection of cash flow, the seasonality of the sales, the elasticity of the production and the flexibility of the company to adapt to the changes that appear during the exercise. The feedback will set the standards to take the pertinent measures.

b. Products in process: using the great advances of industrial engineering, after a conscientious study of methods of work and distribution of the plant, it comes to the measurement of the time of processing.

The optimal amount of units in production is function of the time of process, the capacity of the plant, the prognosis of sales and the number of finished product that are defined as political considering the qualitative aspects.

One recommends special care of the wastes, investigating its causes and taking the remedial actions and reporting it in the state of results.

c. Raw materials: each company should proceed to determine a level of minimum stock as a safety margin, sum to which the amounts will be added to the order, based on the following variables:

- Amount of units to produce
- Standard consumption by each unit to produce.
- The origin of the product (if it is imported, if it is domestic or if it comes from some region different from the location of the plant)
- Available facilities at a given moment, by another one of similar characteristics.
- Commercial relations with the supplier
- Transportation facilities
- Minimum conditions of the supplier (demands as far as minimum orders)

It corresponds to the managing of the storing of raw materials, to determine in accordance with the acquired experience, the safety margins and to process periodic orders, consulting the eventual corrections that are made to the production program.

d. Spare parts: for whose handling all the previous considerations are useful and you specify them according to the types of products.

B. COMMERCIAL COMPANIES: for the companies of this type of handling of the inventories it constitutes altogether with the portfolio, the spinal cord of the managing of the business.

In this type of companies the suitable management of the work capital guarantees optimal results. Among the retailers an affirmation is very common according to which the business becomes by means of the purchase procedure. In the world of the businesses lives a permanent disloyalty for the consumer's money. The experts in marketing teach that consumer is by its changing nature; sometimes rational, other touching and in certain cases sufficiently analytical, etc.

Beginning from a key concept, according to which to predict the behavior of the consumer is a very complex problem and that depends on a great number of variables as the individual behaviors, the buying power, the economic perspective and other variables as much as of macro as micro-economic type which they properly do not constitute the object of this article, we concluded that:

- The combination of this great amount of so divergent variables is the one that really induce to the purchase decision.
- Predicting the right behavior constitutes the main challenge of the retailer. But, as they also say, that it does not obey a mathematical model, but rather to the "sense of smell" or what could be called "commercial ability", in some cases innate and in others acquired based on experience.
- It is specially intended to predict a demand, to make the purchase in the best conditions considering the previously mentioned variables and to verify the success in the prediction. The retailer constantly comes repeating operations of this type. It is a constant handling of risks versus profanity expectation. From the practical point of view, very little has advanced in the measurement of the risk, we can neither offer a formula.
- We again return to invoke a gold rule in the businesses:

PRUDENCE AND GOOD CRITERION: when there is no previous knowledge of the article for how much they it represent true innovation, it will be called on to the industrialist to consider the amount of money that could be frozen or be lost in the event of wrong guessing, without the company suffering an impact in its liquidity, because we always must have as a basic premise, the opportune payment to the suppliers not forgetting that in general terms, the obtaining of a discount by onetime payment constitutes a great investment.

C. AGGRO-INDUSTRIAL COMPANIES: in this sector it is fulfilled in greater proportion with the considerations previously done, and consequently, the use of the criterion and the experience which, are constituted in definite elements to handle controllable or uncontrollable variables according to the case. It is very useful for the economic use of the statistical techniques and projections according to updated information as harvests, shortage, period of production, etc.

2. HANDLING OF STATISTICS

In the administration of inventories because of the so called method of trail and mistake, the detailed and wide accumulation of statistics that record the experiences acquired through time is constituted in a basic and irreplaceable element as help in the decision making process.

Each company will have to design its own models and to complement them with the notes that it considers pertinent to have of elements judgment which facilitate the decision making.

For example it would be possible to be prepared: the monthly sales discriminated by lines of products, by geographic sectors, salesmen; notes on advertising campaigns, change of price, sales offers, production per hectares; fertilizer ranges per/m^2; number of bushels per block, etc.

With the accumulation of data and the use of the technique of the inference statistical (prediction) the measurement of elasticity of the demand in relation to the different variables can be tried, as the price and the publicity, indicators of correlation; models of regression, etc. providing elements of judgment as important support to measure the results of the decisions to be made, and to try to predict the behavior of the demand, that as we said previously, constitutes the variable key for the management of inventories.

3. HANDLING ASPECTS

The concept of responsibility centers is very useful. A zoning of the different types of inventories are recommended in such a way that for all products, a person in charge and respond for the amount in stock loses by theft and deterioration and for their conservation and handling of the products.

The distribution by areas obeys to measurable rules from the point of view of industrial engineering, that is to say, they do not respond to the operational control.

Consequently, it should be done based in the administrative control, considering among others the following variables:

- Amount of orders / days.
- Easiness of manipulation, according to the packing, weight and specific conditions.
- Physical distribution of the warehouses.
- Necessity of special care to avoid the deterioration.
- Product homogeneity to group in an area.

The ones in charge of each area have the responsibility to handle it as if it was their own business, because they are responsible for it. It will be his commitment to warn when the product arrives at the indicated level is replaced for they must take care of the case, the requirements by computer or roll o decks cards.

Also they must be responsible for a suitable manipulation to maintain the goods in optimal conditions and to be responsible for any loss that happens. The salesmen must prepare the orders by areas; and the director of purchases will come in the same way, entering the information of inventor is which a codification in accordance e with the requirements for each business.

By the accumulation of experiences, the company can to distribute in equitable form the different centers, with the object of maintaining the personnel occupied, with balanced loads. As example areas in a commercial company it can be insinuated:

Area 1: Footwear
Area 2: Household-electric
Area 3: Ironworks Articles and other

Area 4: Toy store
Area 5: Articles for the home
Area 6: Preparations

4. METHODS OF COSTS

The accounting presents/displays many methods of costs, among most important there are:

A. FIFO: according to which, the first units entering the inventory, will be the first in leaving. According to this method the materials that are being used pay for the oldest price of acquisition increasing the contribution margin.

B. LIFO: last in entering, first out. The used materials are loaded on to the most recent price, reducing the profit margin.

C. COST AVERAGE: the average calculates a value, that is to say, the units are paid for base on the arithmetic average of the prices of acquisition.

D. NEPS: next in entering, first in leaving; it is equivalent to a value of replacement; in other words, the price to replace it.

E. SPECIFIED COST: as the case of the cars or businesses of real estate.

Note: As far as possible to the value of the raw materials the handling cost is due to be added until its location in plant (loads, insurances, transport, etc.)

If it must pay a superior tax to the one recognized by the government, this greater value must be added to the material; if the expenses are not perfectly identifiable they enter as indirect expenses of manufacture.

For industrial companies it is possible to be used costing by absorption or direct costing. The basic difference between both methods is based in the processing of fixed the indirect costs of manufacture, renting, administration, etc.

Direct costing assumes that these costs appear based on time and consequently they are not accumulated as a greater value of the produced units. This way the units paid for by the absorption method are overvalued in relation to costs by direct system.

Let us remember that if in a period of time the produced and sold units are equal, the earnings statements are identical by both methods of costing and that direct costing is especially recommendable for purely administrative effects and specific businesses, especially when the plant capacity has not been reached. The combination of both methods is very recommendable form an agreement.

Each company will use the system of costing as more recommendable for its specific situation, considering the advantages and disadvantages to each one of the methods enunciated previously.

For control effects, the periodic processing of physical inventories is indispensable to confront with the standard firing dates and to take the appropriate actions, as much managerial (identifying the people in charge) as accountable.

If the loses appear by managing faults they are considered a cost; if by inherent causes to the product or the process, on costs of the product and in the other cases, they can be treated as indirect expenses of manufacture.

5. USE OF THE COMPUTERS

With the extraordinary advance of the technology of the computers, among others, specific models of handling of inventories have been developed, which ease up the accumulation of statistics by the great capacity of information storage, the key variable in the use of experiences.

Equally important, is the great facility of consultation, using the different measures from exit of information, besides to offer basic accuracy and promptness, elements for the decision making.

The companies use software for control of inventories. This one begins with an account of inventories in its memory; these programs only work feeding them with:

- Physical inventory
- Purchases
- Price of purchase per article (code)
- Sale price per article (code)
- Percentage that is paid in taxes

As of a sale made, from the cash register properly connected to a terminal, it is recorded by the computer and it immediately makes the unloading of or articles.

The advantages this kind of software offer are as follows:

- It permits an immediate and updated knowledge of the inventory.
- It reduces considerably the costs of the handling of the inventory.
- When the non singular sale it is made the unloading is also made not only on the accounting but also in the inventory making it more agile and efficient.
- It establishes very important statistics for the making of decisions, as for example the average of the purchases, the price average, the percentage in which the prices of purchase varies, etc.
- When one has handled these systems, by a year or more it allows to create statistics that inform on the periods in which there is greater rotation of inventories, which kind of articles are sold in greater number at different times, which tendency do the prices have in certain product shortage etc.
- It allows creating standards of minimum and maximum inventory of each product individually, and an inventory average that is due to have at a certain time or period. This software, as it always maintains updated the inventory, has a very important option if a minimum level of each one of products paid attention; to at the moment at which it is arrived at the minimum amount of inventory of an article, it gives a warning so that an order is put in.

With respect to the advantages that this class of software offers, one is due to stand out that the exact and immediate information that the program offers, to make fast decisions. Let us remember, when the company has greater and better information this in competitive advantage with respect to the other companies. For example, when they pay standards attention it can be anticipated ahead of time low inventories of certain products, or also the stagnation of certain kind of goods in a period, easing up the decision making.

Takes advantage witch the information of the data bases that throws software to know are the best periods for purchases, to determine the level of optimal inventory.

CHAPTER 9

MODEL OF INVENTORIES

by josavere

1. USE OF COMPUTERS

With the extraordinary advance of technology and of computers, which have developed specific models of handling of inventories and the accumulation of statistics for great information-storage capacity, variable make key in the utilization of experiences. Is very important for the great counseling facility, to use every mean possible for the display of information (visual display screen, diskette, CD, printed matter), in addition to offer exactness and promptness, basic elements.

The companies utilize software of inventory control. This begins with a physical count of units and his record in the software, feeding it with data like:

- Inventory
- Purchase price for article (code)
- Sales price for article (code)
- Percentage that is paid in taxes

To measure than of he does a sale, from the box properly connected to a terminal, he gets registered for the computer and immediately makes the discharge of the goods.

The advantages that offer this software are:

a. It permits an immediate knowledge and updated of the inventory at any time.

b. Reduce considerably the costs of the handling of the inventory.

c. When the sale comes true not only has he done the discharge in the inventory but also in bookkeeping doing it more agile and efficient.

d. It establishes very important statistics for the overtaking for example, the average of the shopping that they vary the purchase prices, etc, the average price, and the percentage.

e. The experience using these systems permits creating statistics that inform on the periods that is bigger inventory, the goods more sales in different epochs, than tendency have the pricing in determined periods and epochs of scarcity of certain products, etc.

f. It permits creating standards of minimum inventory and peak out of every product in particular and an average inventory that it should be had in an epoch or determined period. This software, as maintains always updated the inventory, has a very important option if a minimal level out of every one of products has been fixed; the moment that it take place to the minimum inventory of an article immediately order an buy.

Regarding the advantages, the software can offer the exact and immediate information, so you can take action faster. Let's remember, when the company has information, better is the competitive advantage regarding them besides companies. For example, when they fix standards remaining of given products can be foreseen ahead of time, or also the stagnation of certain goods in a period, making easy the decisions.

Also the information takes advantage of databases that the software for Knowledge throws, as periods for shopping are better, determining the level of optimal inventory, among others.

2. INVENTORIES, A DYNAMIC MODEL (josavere)

A model tries to find that I allow to us the request (or production, as the case may be) without falling in excesses but without losing sales or giving up producing for lack of finished product or of available raw materials.

Utilizing excel we can do a simple and easy program to apply that we described using some input and combining with some formulas that indicate step by step.

a. A database with all of the goods that fix the portfolio is prepared, registering the consumption of three last months (month to month).

A1: D22

Description (A)	January (B)	February (C)	March (D)	Total (E)	Paretic. Cons. (%) (F)	Average Working day (G)	I.F. March (H)	Paretic. Exist. (%) (I)	Days Exist (J)	Lead Time (K)
A	330	333	438	1,101	24.5	15	464	25.2	31.2	45
B	234	215	300	749	16.6	10	5	0.3	0.5	5
C	117	180	152	449	10.0	6	12	0.7	2.0	30
D	105	85	118	308	6.9	4	132	7.1	31.6	15
E	73	82	144	299	6.6	4	171	9.3	42.2	15
F	100	80	82	262	5.8	4	286	15.5	80.9	45
G	79	79	84	242	5.4	3	27	2.0	11.5	5
H	90	72	65	227	5.1	3	106	5.7	34.3	45
I	52	55	99	206	4.6	3	106	5.7	37.8	30
J	44	56	86	186	4.1	3	193	10.5	76.5	60
K	46	42	42	130	2.9	2	16	0.9	9.2	5
L	42	38	45	125	2.8	2	162	8.8	96.1	45
M	29	26	25	80	1.7	1	93	5.1	92.4	45
N	13	17	24	54	1.2	1	1	0.0	0.4	5
O	12	9	18	39	0.9	1	15	0.8	27.7	5
P	9	2	22	33	0.7	1	24	1.3	54.3	5
Q	4	0	3	7	0.2	1	18	1.0	192.4	5
R	0	1	3	4	0.1	1	0	0.0	0.0	15
S	3	1	1	5	0.1	1	3	0.2	64.7	5
Total:	1,382	1,373	1,751	4,506	100	66	1,834	100		

b. The consumption of three months under consideration to calculate the Consumption of the trimester consolidates (E = B + C + D).

c. Calculates him the average daily consumed in the last ones three months dividing the consumption of the trimester for the number of working days (G = E / # of working days).

d. He shares the total of the consumption of three months (column E) of every article, among the grand total of inventory to estimate the percentage participation of every item around consumption (F = E1 / E20).

e. Orders him the column principle's F to minor (looking for the Pareto principle).

f. They insert themselves like in - put, or input data, the numbers of existence, according to physical inventory at final of the trimester (column H).

g. Dividing the column the H for F (consume per day) calculates dais's number which we have supplying for itself (J = H / G).

h. In the column K, registered input data the number of days that we needed to be replenished by the supplier, addend amount that we having like buffer stock for any eventuality (Lead time).

i. Utilizing the tool Conditional format we give the following instructions: If column J is inferior, to column K, mark with red (alert little India), the column J.

j. In the same way, utilizing conditional format, we compared J (days which we have supplying for), with participation in consumption (column F). If the participation of consumption is superior to participation in supplies also we marked with red.

k. We took care of initially the goods that search two reds (critical zone) and we went on with the ones that registered one to make a decision, backing them up in the information of the model.

l. One proceeds for the month following inserting the data of the latter month and omitting the first month, thus:

- January—March—February
- February—March—April
- April—May—June
- June—July—August

And so on like he can see oneself in the example:

Description (A)	February (B)	March (C)	April (D)	Total (E)	Paretic. Cons. (%) (F)	Average Working day (G)	I.F. March (H)	Paretic. Exist. (%) (I)	Days Exist (J)	Lead Time (K)
A	334	43	369	746	18.0	10	565	28.0	56	45
B	215	300	171	686	16.6	9	16	0.8	2	5
C	180	152	139	467	11.3	6	21	1.0	3	30
D	85	118	95	298	7.2	4	108	5.4	27	15
E	83	144	67	294	7.1	4	134	6.6	34	15
F	80	82	130	292	7.1	4	376	18.6	95	45
G	79	84	75	238	5.7	3	37	1.8	12	5
H	72	65	52	189	4.6	3	78	3.9	31	45
I	55	99	88	242	5.8	3	107	5.3	33	30
J	56	86	63	205	5.0	3	216	10.7	78	60
K	42	42	64	148	3.6	2	10	0.5	5	5
L	39	45	43	126	3.0	2	131	6.5	77	45
M	26	25	22	73	1.8	1	140	6.9	142	45
N	17	24	8	49	1.2	1	1	0.0	2	5
O	9	18	9	36	0.9	0	29	1.4	60	5
P	2	22	9	33	0.8	0	29	1.4	65	5
Q	0	3	3	6	0.1	0	15	0.7	185	5
R	1	3	6	10	0.2	0	0	0.0	0	15
S	1	1	1	3	0.1	0	4	0.2	99	5
Total:	1,375	1,356	1,41	4,141	100	56	2,017	100		

Description (A)	March (B)	April (C)	May (D)	Total (E)	Paretic. Cons. (%) (F)	Average Working day (G)	I.F. March (H)	Paretic. Exist. (%) (I)	Days Exist (J)	Lead Time (K)
A	438	369	336	1,143	26.0	15	231	14.5	15	45
B	300	171	184	655	14.9	9	1	0.1	0	5
C	152	135	114	401	9.1	5	12	0.8	2	30
D	118	95	65	278	6.3	4	99	6.2	26	15
E	144	67	79	290	6.6	4	220	13.9	56	15
F	82	130	69	281	6.4	4	307	19.3	81	45
G	84	75	69	228	5.2	3	40	2.5	13	5
H	65	52	45	162	3.7	2	57	3.6	26	45
I	99	88	60	247	5.6	3	56	3.5	17	30
J	86	63	47	196	4.5	3	212	13.4	80	60
K	42	64	47	153	3.5	2	12	0.8	6	5
L	45	43	41	129	2.9	2	135	8.5	77	45
M	25	22	23	70	1.6	1	117	7.4	124	45
N	24	8	8	40	0.9	1	1	0.1	2	5
O	18	9	19	46	1.0	1	45	2.8	72	5
P	22	9	13	44	1.0	1	31	2.0	52	5
Q	3	3	4	10	0.2	0	11	0.7	81	5
R	3	6	2	11	0.3	0	0	0.0	0	15
S	1	1	6	8	0.2	0	1	0.1	9	5
Total:	1,751	1,41	1,231	4,392	100	59	1,588	100		

Equally important he is to employ us of the goods that they find themselves stored in shelves and do not register movement with a good opinion, we can establish suchlike reports:

Days without consumption	Article	Quantity	Value	Percentage
60 - 90				
90 - 110				
120 - 180				
< - 180				

The previous model must be interpreted as a guide or auxiliary mathematics, in order to make the overtaking of decisions; is essential the executive's good opinion.

CHAPTER 10

WORKING CAPITAL

by josavere

It is defined as the difference between current assets and current liabilities or also as the proportion of current assets financed with long-term funds.

	Assets	Passive
Work Capital {	Current Assets	Current Passive
	Fixed Assets	Passives Length Term
		Patrimony

$$CT = AC - PC$$

According to basic principles of finance, working capital is the equivalent to the minimum of current assets (cash, banks, temporary investments, accounts receivables and inventories) that a company must finance with its own resources or with long term debt or with a contribution.

In an economy that is rapidly changing, the great advances in telecommunications have shortened the distances and some of the principles stated by the classical economist questioned because they never thought of radical change in the businesses people.

Working capital is defined as the assets and liabilities that can be turned into cash in a period of time of less than one year. For practical purposes it is more logical to define the short term as the time for the operative cycle of the company. In other words the period of time between the buying of r a w materials and the collection of accounts receivables, this short term will have a variable duration depending of the type of business for financial purposes.

Current assets are:

a. Cash and banks
b. Temporary investments
c. Accounts receivable
d. Inventories:

- Raw materials
- Work in process
- Finished good

The productive cycle starts buying raw materials, adding value to them through the accumulation of direct and indirect material; the use of labor and obtaining a finished product which is sold usually on credit afterwards. Those receivables are collected at the cost and obtaining a profit, this cycle repeats self. If the product sells with a good margin a profit is obtained and liquidity is looked for.

This liquidity allows the company to buy materials in optimal terms (Prompt delivery, good prices, good quality, and discounts for early payments) allowing the corporation efficiency in its plant capacity, improves its productivity, reduce costs and be able to compete in the market with competitive prices.

Liquidity and profitability are very close related. The only time when this relationship is questioned is when a corporation does not have analyzed enough its projected cash flows.

If we have a good stimulation of the inflows and outflows of cash, all excess liquidity means a reduction of profitability to the amount that those excesses could be put to gain interest instead of helping, then without earning anything.

On the contrary, deficit means the risk of not being able to pay and increase financial mistake which bring the lost of managerial capacity.

Generally, financial writers have two assumptions:

- Short term money is cheaper than long term money
- Current assets are less profitable than fix assets

Now we are going to discuss these two assumptions in order learn how to deal with the situation.

In relation to the first assumption, short-term money sometimes has been much more expensive than long term money. The second assumption brings all doubts. First for all, the assumption has some logic because the fix assets should be more profitable than current assets, of the contrary nobody build infrastructure, people simply would put the money in a financial institution.

Only with the interchanging of fix and current assets could be possible to add value and earn a profit. What is important then is to define the proportion of each assets; this is known as asset structure.

The most modern equipment, located at the modern facility by them does not genera a profit. Only, when **are operated by people** using the best material and the rights products can do it.

Based on the prior analysis we can conclude that the projection of cash flow is a basic to manage the working capital to the company. The following are some of the principles used to calculate the cash flow.

1. Only those transactions that have inflows or outflows are taken in consideration also, the date of occurrence.

2. After finishing the projections, a careful review of the payments must be made and special attention and should be put into capital authorization and interest expenses.

3. In the outflow section, a degree of occurrence is expected, because liabilities have to be paid in predetermined dates.

4. In relation to inflows caution is recommended a new assumption that your customers will pay on time. The best way to project this is to use historical data or use all the experience the company has in this field.

All this considerations help to build a conservative cash flow budget; it is better to be conservative than optimistic, it is much easier to put money to earn interest than go out and get funds in a short notice.

Don´t forget to treat financial numbers which are only one part of the analysis, some quantitative aspects become very important when the cash flow budget is going to be approved.

In inflationary economies, it is recommended to work with standard costs in order to maintain the buying power of the exports as prices of raw materials increases reacquiring increments in working capital.

Inflation is a discrete variable and can be easily programmed in our electronic page where we are doing the projections. In periods of inflation it is recommended a faster depreciation, cost system using LIFO and being conservative in applying the accounting principles.

Using these principles the director of the company could present an estimate of earnings, therefore he will have less pressure to announce dividends and beside he will pay fewer taxes. He will indexes sacrifice in the short term such as return on equity but retain a good level of working capital needed to fight against inflationary pressures.

From the managerial it is very important to attain levels of working capital by turnover; while more profits are obtained with money that has the same buying power from the least effect with the inflation. The accounting system must be simple enough to differentiate between speculative and earnings from operations.

1. FACTORS THAT AFFECT WORKING CAPITAL

A. TYPE OF BUSINESS: this is a very important factor and is related to the financial capacity of the owners or investors profit. Some types of business practically does not need working capital because their generation of cash is very easy.

B. PRODUCTIVE CYCLE AND UNIT COST: the shorter, the productive cycle and the lower cost, the lower is the working capital. It need less working capital to manufacture underwear women's that men's suits.

C. SALES VOLUME: obviously, more capital is needed when there is more amount of sales.

D. BUYING AND SALES TERMS: the manufacturer can be using its supplies reacquiring less working capital.

E. INVENTORY TURNOVER AND ACCOUNTS RECEIVABLES: if the cash turnover faster, less working capital.

F. CYCLE OF THE BUSINESSES: it relates to the general conditions of macroeconomic type. When the economy works well is much easier to obtain credit and therefore less is required working capital. It is very important to remember that type of situations is temporary and it demands caution of the management.

G. SEASONALITY OF THE SALES: while the more stable are the sales, easier it is to assemble a cycle of production (purchases) and to obtain a high level of efficiency, trimming the productive cycle and at the same time reducing the necessity of working capital. On the opposite case, it agrees to combine with products of opposite seasonality in order to stabilize the level of income.

Chapter 11

FINANCIAL ANALYSIS

by josavere

INTRODUCTION

The financial analysis constitutes a tool of lots of analytic usefulness. It allows us to make relative comparisons of different businesses and facility decisions of investment, finances, action plans, control of operations and dividends distribution

A generalized series of financial reasons exist. As a base of this article we will use the formulas commonly used by he recognized authors in this matter.

1. GENERAL PRESENTATION

We can speak about five aspects of the analysis: liquidity, activity, indebtedness, yield, cover and we complement them with EVA (index of value generation, witch, because of its importance is treated in a separate chapter).

We will make an initial presentation; then we will indicate their limitations and afterwards we will do, complementary analyses for their better use are suggested. At the end of the document one example is given.

A. LIQUIDITY: measure the capacity of the companies to cancel their short term obligations. They help to establish the facility or difficulty that a company has to pay its current passive with the product to turn into cash its working capital. It helps to determine what would happen if the immediate payment of all its obligations in less than a year were demanded.

We have the following indexes:

    a.   Captital of work = current active - current passive (monetary units)

It expresses in amount that the current reason display as a relation. It indicates the value that would be left to the company, represented in current cash or other liabilities, after paying all its short term liabilities, in case that they had to be cancelled immediately.

    b.   Current reason = $\dfrac{\text{current active}}{\text{current passive}}$ (times)

It indicates the relationship between the current active and the short term liabilities

    c.   Acid test = $\dfrac{\text{current active - inventories}}{\text{current passive}}$ (times)

It reveals the capacity of the company to cancel its current obligations, but without counting on the sale of its supplies, basically with the balances of cash, the product of its accounts to receive, its temporary investments and some other actives of easy liquidation, different from the inventories.

It is a relationship similar to the previous one but without considering the inventories.

    d.   EBITDA = Operative profit + Depreciation + Amortization + provisions

B. ACTIVITY: constitute an important complement of the liquidity reasons. They measure the duration of the productive cycle and the period of portfolio. The following indicators are used:

    a.   Rotation of inventories = $\dfrac{\text{cost of sold merchandise}}{\text{inventory average}}$

The inventory of merchandise of a company rotates X times during the year, this means, that the inventory becomes X times cash per year or accounts to receive.

b. Average of inventory = $\dfrac{360 \text{ days}}{\text{rotation of inventories}}$

It is equivalent to the previous relationship but expressed in days.

c. Rotation of accounts to receive = $\dfrac{\text{annual on credit sales}}{\text{average of C x C}}$

Establishes the number of times that the accounts to receive turn in average on a determined period of time, generally a year.

d. Average of accounts to receive = $\dfrac{360 \text{ days}}{\text{rotation of C x C}}$

It indicates the number of days that the accounts to receive take to rotate.

e. Rotation of annual accounts to pay = $\dfrac{\text{annual buys on credit}}{\text{average of C x P}}$

It indicates the number of times that the accounts to pay turn in a certain period.

f. Average of accounts to pay = $\dfrac{360 \text{ days}}{\text{rotation of C x P}}$

It provides a clue of the general average of days that the company spends to cancel its accounts.

g. Rotation of actives = $\dfrac{\text{annual sales}}{\text{total actives}}$

The total actives rotated X times during the year, or each dollar invested in actives generated sales for U.S. $X in the year.

C. INDEBTEDNESS (LEVERAGE): it shows the participation of a third party in the capital of the company. The following indexes are calculated:

$$\text{a. Reason of indebtedness} = \frac{\text{total passive}}{\text{total active}}$$

For each dollar that the company has invested in actives, $X has been financed by the creditors, or that the creditors are owners of X% of the company and the shareholders owners of the complement.

$$\text{b. Reason of passive liabilities to capital} = \frac{\text{long term passive}}{\text{equity}}$$

For each dollar of the patrimony long term commitments are had for $X, so, each dollar of the owners is long term compromised in X%.

$$\text{c. Index of passive debt of capitalization} = \frac{\text{long term passive}}{\text{Long term passive} + \text{equity}}$$

It is a complementary version of the index of total indebtedness; it shows the importance that the long term debt has on the structure of capital of the company. It indicates % of the long term structure that is represented by the debt with a third.

D. COVER: it measures the capacity of the company to cover the fix charges (interests)

$$\text{a. Times that the interests have been gained} = \frac{\text{UAII}}{\text{annual payment of interest}}$$

It indicates if the company generates during the period a profit before taxes and interest X times superior to interests paid. This means, if the company generates enough profits to pay interests superior to the present ones.

b. Cover of fixed charges = $\dfrac{\text{UAII}}{\text{annual payment of interest} + \dfrac{(1) \text{ amortizations of capital}}{1-t}}$

(1)=UAII: profits before interests and taxes
t: rate of taxes

E. YIELD: measure the productivity of the funds compromised in a business. Let us remember that at long term the important thing is to guarantee the permanence of the company in market increment and therefore its value. It allows us to watch the behavior of the company in comparison with the sales and the capital.

a. Gross margin of profit = $\dfrac{\text{gross profit}}{\text{gross sales}}$

It means that the sales of the company generated an X% of profits during the year. In other words, each dollar sold during the year generated $X of net profit.

b. Net margin of profit = $\dfrac{\text{net profits}}{\text{net sales}}$

The net profit corresponds to an X% of the sales during the year, that is to say, that each dollar sold generates $X of net profit during the year.

c. Yield of the investment = $\dfrac{\text{net profit}}{\text{equity}}$

The profits corresponded to X% on the patrimony during the year; it indicates what corresponds to the partners as yield on their investment.

d. Potential of profit = margin x rotation =

$$\text{Margin x Rotation} = \frac{\text{net profit}}{\text{net sales}} \times \frac{\text{net sales}}{\text{total active}}$$

It shows that it is the same to say, that the net profit with respect to the total actives like an annual percentage, and that each dollar invested in the total active generated \$X of net profit during the year.

F. INDICATORS OF VALUE GENERATION:

a. $EVA = \dfrac{U}{P} - CC$

    U: Profits
    P: equity
    CC: cost of capital

If the company is generating Value EVA it must be superior to 0. If EVA is inferior to 0 (Negative) the company is destroying value. We refer widely to this indicator in another document.

b. Corrected and projected EVACp (josavere):

$$EVAC_p \text{ (josavere)} = \frac{U + I\&D + Po + PMA}{P + A} - CC$$

    $EVAC_p$: corrected and projected EVA
    U: profit of the period
    I&D: investments & development
    Po: positions
    PMA: environment preservation
    CC: cost of capital
    P: equity
    A: adjustments to the equity

2. LIMITATIONS

A. LIQUIDITY: an imperfection of the traditional analysis consists on ignoring the deadlines of the passives. Arbitrarily it is defined as of long term one that expires in a term superior to a year and as of short terms the rest.

According to this classification it is considered the same a debt that expires the following day of the date of the balance, that one that expires 359 days later.

The continuity principle, supposes that the society has indefinite life, unless the opposite is said specifically, Hendriksen, affirms that liquidity should not be measured by the amount of current assets, because it is assuming that the company is being eliminated, which is not correct most of the times. The important thing is to analyze the capacity of the company to generate cash in the normal course of the business.

The account to receive involves two factors. In the first place, who sell on credit takes the risk that some accounts could not be paid by the indebted; in the second place, is very common that some clients are delayed in their payments. About the accounting information it is not possible to be deduced how liquid are the receive accounts; detailed analysis of all the clients is required to be able to draw a conclusion.

The inventories represent a worthy factor to analyze with all the caution needed. We can make three classifications: raw materials, product in process and finished product. This last one is next to come in a way of a payment that the previous ones and, the raw material can be more liquid than the product in process. The financial analysis considers them equally liquid.

The quantity of inventories depends between other aspects of the used estimate methods, that can be FIFO (first units in entering, first in leaving), LIFO (last units in entering, last in leaving); average, specific cost.

Finally, if a careful classification does not appear, it would be ignoring the different problems that can be displayed: Obsolescence, fashion changes, deterioration, oversupply, etc. As a rescuing formula appears the acid test, which can give one a very deceptive calculation in certain cases such as, would be a supermarket, business that by its nature displays very liquid inventories in most of the cases.

B. ACTIVITY: the cost of the merchandise depends on the system of valuation used for the inventories and its number average is very little representative when they are businesses with stationary sales.

In the portfolio rotation, more over to the imprecision mentioned in liquidity, we can say, that the average of accounts to receive is little representative when they are businesses that display a concentration of sales at certain times.

C. INDEBTEDNESS: in order to calculate the reason total active/total debt, in the numerator the deadline of the liabilities is ignored, very important characteristic in inflationary economies.

The total active, in most cases the figures of balance change considerably with relation to the real value. The current part it's already sufficiently analyzed; the stable portion, in almost the totality of the cases is sub valued.

In effect, about the machinery and equipment, we found in the balance an equivalent value in books at the cost of acquisition except the accumulated depreciation.

Due to the inflationary problem, when it is national capital goods or the devaluation of the money with relation to the dollar in the case of imputed goods, generally while the actives serve economically, its value is increased based on current money, the same for register sales.

In greater proportion the phenomenon appears witch the lands, that not even accountable are depreciated and that by the phenomenon of restricted supply with an increasing demand, increase their value in constant dollars (considering the loss of the buying power of the money). With the constructions that have so long useful life a very similar phenomenon happens.

D. COVER: these indicators are affected by the same way to those of yield. For these indexes of analysis of the internal generation of cash flow is critical.

E. YIELD: the main problem of the conceptual type. The accounting in most of the cases recognizes the profit at the moment of the sale.

The rent is generated through all the productive cycle, including the activities of buying of raw materials and collection of portfolio. Also, the value of the profit depends to the accounting policies about depreciations, amortizations, valuations of inventories, punishments of portfolios, etc.

The value of the equity (total active - total passive), is considerably affected by the observations previously done in relation to the actives, passives and very specially, by the value of the intangible ones that in many cases constitute a highly representative figure in proportion to the total of actives of the company.

3. HOW TO IMPROVE THE FINANCIAL INFORMATION

The fundamental thing is that the analyst has a clear knowledge about the previously listed limitations. We have to look for information about the company, its partners, their products, their consumers, system of distribution, competitors, etc. Accepting as a great limitation of general type in the analysis, its character of static, because it is done base on a cut of accounts to the date, it is recommendable that analyzes the financial situation by the use of a representative number of balance (minimum three) in order to observe the tendency that shows the different indicators and hopefully base on projected financial statements if the decisions are oriented to the future.

A. LIQUIDITY: the idea is to study the projection of the cash flow. This has a dynamic character and it allows seeing with clarity if the company in its normal operation it's in conditions to honor its commitments on time, as it corresponds to the objective of the financial function.

Before calculating the current reason, it is recommendable to analyze the portfolio and to exclude the accounts of doubtful collection and those that are considered losses. About the number of inventories we must make a careful classification that allows us to see if they comprise or not the characteristic of quality, if some supplies are obsolete or old-fashioned, if the supplies are enough or if on the contrary excesses appear. Moreover, we have to examine the criterion of valuation used and its effect on the used indicators.

The accounts to pay constitute a certain number at the moment of the analysis. It is important to consider that the due date plays a definitive role to estimate the present value, which is ignored in the financial analysis. An account with deadline in few days more than 360 must be included as current.

The EBITDA must be related to the net sale and be expressed in percentage.

These considerations made we proceed to calculate the **refined test (josavere)**. This does not obey to a specific formula. It is characterized essentially by being, of good criterion on the part of the analyst, to calculate the times that the realizable active covers the current passive in a specific moment. This test emphasizes in the capacity to generate funds by the normal activity of the company. For example, we could calculate it by the following formula:

$$P \text{ of josavere} = \frac{AC - [\text{Production in Process} + \text{Portfolio (to more than 180 days)}^{1}]}{\text{Current Passive}}$$

B. ACTIVITY: we must review carefully the method of estimation of the inventories to determine the cost of the merchandise sold. In order to determine the average of accounts as a receipt and inventories, it is recommended to use the appropriate statistical measurement as indicator of the central tendency (average, mode, medium), complementing it with dispersion indicators.

As far as possible the averages are due to calculate base on the monthly figures, especially if they are seasonal sales. If the data presents much dispersion the medium one is preferable. If relative concentration exists the mode is more recommendable, than the average Arithmetic.

As far as portfolio it is very advisable to ask for aging or decaying of the total by past due date. Empirically it has been possible to conclude that the older the account, the more difficult it is its collection.

C. INDEBTEDNESS: before entering to calculate indexes it is recommendable to update the figures of balance bringing the actives to real value. In the case of current actives, the situation has been sufficiently analyzed. For the stable active a technical estimate conducted by experts is desirable. As far as the debt, it agrees to calculate the net present value in according the model of financial mathematics.

---

[1] Assuming that neither the product in process nor the portfolio with more than 180 days are easily attainable in the particular case.

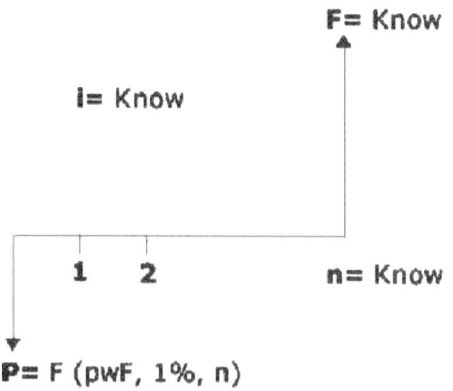

D. COVER: in order to calculate these indexes the same observations analyzed for the yield indicators are valid, recommending the use of the indicator of total cover because it considers the amortizations of the debt.

In general for the investment decisions, valuation of companies, alternatives of financing, absorptions and fusions, it is recommended to work with indicators calculated based on the projections of the company and very specially the calculation of EVACp to which, given its importance we talked about in another chapter.

E. YIELD: before taking the figure from profits an analysis of qualitative type is recommendable. In the first place we must separate the operative profit of the occasional, of possession or both.

Of course, the yield indexes are due to calculate according to the operative profit and must be subjected to the internal generation of cash flow; the profits obtained by yield of other investments and by accomplishment of assets must separately be analyzed. In a specific moment, the accomplishment of assets can be a great decision of managerial, as also it can be at the moment of the investment. The important, at the moment of the sale, consists of taking care of the fulfillment of the basic objective of the financial function: permanent generation of value to increase the value of share in the market with high indexes on stock-exchange.

At the time of making a financial decision a great risk is taken if the internal financial analysis is only considered (own organization), because it is not possible not known that other types of factors exist that obviously affect the performance of the companies, as it is the enterprise group to that belong, the sector in which they develop, the domestic and international economic situation, by this the indexes are due to consider that to calculate on the factors previously mentioned, since it would be possible to be spoken of a financial analysis of the enterprise reality that is being lived; otherwise the financial decisions would be bad, because it would be losing vision of the present financial position of the company in the economy.

Finance for Non-Financiers 1

HERYO S.A
(Amounts in million pesos)

BALANCE SHEET

	Basic 0 Year	Vertical Analysis %	Year I	Vertical Analysis. %	Horizontal Analysis (I-0)/0 %	Year II	Analysis VERT. %	HORIZ (II-I)/I %	Year III	Analysis VERT. %	HORIZ. (III-II)/II %	Year IV	Analysis VERT. %	HORIZ. (IV-III)/III %
ACTIVE														
CURRENTE ASSETS														
Available	4,000	0.01	6,766	0.01	0.69	9,505	0.01	0.40	10,442	0.012	0.10	12,270	0.014	0.18
Investments	1,851	0.00	500	0.00	-0.73	0		-1.00	115	0.000	0.00	417	0.000	0.00
Deudores	41,548	0.06	32,951	0.04	-0.21	47,823	0.06	0.45	69,774	0.082	0.46	74,441	0.085	0.07
Inventories	35,592	0.05	40,374	0.04	0.13	51,094	0.07	0.27	58,769	0.069	0.15	70,355	0.080	0.20
Deferred	792	0.00	516	0.00	-0.35	637	0.00	0.23	698	0.001	0.10	629	0.001	-0.10
TOTAL CURRENTE ASSETS	83,783	0.12	81,107	0.09	-0.03	109,059	0.15	0.34	139,798	0.164	0.28	158,112	0.180	0.13
NON CURRENTE ASSETS														
Debtors	257	0.00	4,152	0.00	15.16	7,959	0.01	0.92	3,876	0.005	-0.51	9,819	0.011	1.53
Plant and Equipment Property	49,125	0.07	71,294	0.08	0.45	83,223	0.11	0.17	85,207	0.100	0.02	12,811	0.129	0.32
Appreciation Property. Plant and	68,923	0.10	78,135	0.09	0.13	69,521	0.09	-0.11	79,520	0.093	0.14	92,311	0.105	0.16
Investment	146,278	0.22	291,789	0.32	0.99	299,479	0.40	0.03	341,977	0.401	0.14	360,793	0.412	0.06
Investment Appreciation	318,200	0.47	382,813	0.42	0.20	174,905	0.23	-0.54	195,202	0.229	0.12	141,187	0.161	-0.28
Intangibles	6,275	0.01	6,032	0.01	-0.04	7,011	0.01	0.16	6,298	0.007	-0.10	233	0.000	-0.96
Other Assets	104	0.00	122	0.00	0.17	186	0.00	0.52	219	0.000	0.18	246	0.000	0.12
Appreciation Other Assets	484	0.00	583	0.00	0.20	678	0.00	0.16	730	0.001	0.08	816	0.001	0.12
TOTAL NON CURRENTE ASSETS	589,646	0.88	834,920	0.91	0.42	642,962	0.85	-0.23	713,029	0.836	0.11	18,216	0.820	0.01
TOTAL ASSETS	673,429	100.0%	916,027	100%	0.36	752,021	100.0%	-0.18	852,827	100.0%	0.13	876,328	100.0%	0.03
PASSIV														
CURRENT LIABILITIES														
Financial Obligations	17,663	0.026	22,956	0.025	0.30	21,892	0.03	-0.06	35,766	0.042	0.65	53,454	0.061	0.49
Related	10,116	0.015	9,184	0.010	-0.09	40,983	0.05	3.46	41,925	0.049	0.02	58,486	0.067	0.40
Accounts Payable	13,367	0.020	13,324	0.015	0.00	20,857	0.03	0.57	23,207	0.027	0.11	24,073	0.027	0.04
Taxes, levies and fees	641	0.001	673	0.001	0.05	3,437	0.00	4.11	2,759	0.003	-0.20	8,388	0.010	2.04
Obligaciones laborales	3,111	0.005	3,813	0.004	0.23	4,855	0.01	0.27	6,192	0.007	0.28	6,872	0.008	0.11
Liabilities and Provisions	777	0.001	1,333	0.001	0.72	1,506	0.00	0.13	1,587	0.002	0.05	2,030	0.002	0.28
Deferred	148	0.000	80	0.000	-0.46	20	0.00	-0.75	2,609	0.003	129.45	2,615	0.003	0.00
TOTAL CURRENT LIABILITIES	45,823	6.80%	51,363	0.056	0.12	93,350	0.12	0.82	114,045	0.134	0.22	55,918	0.178	0.37
NON CURRENT LIABILITIES														
Financial Obligations	15,718	2.3%	26,153	0.029	0.66	17,061	0.02	-0.35	18,719	0.022	0.10	10,048	0.011	-0.46
Labor Obligations	273	0.00	199	0.000	-0.27			-1.00	0	0.000	0.00	0	0.000	0.00
Accrued Liabilities and Provisions	4,498	0.01	6,378	0.007	0.42	7,503	0.01	0.18	8,952	0.010	0.19	9,324	0.011	0.04
Deferred	173	0.00	123	0.000	-0.29	123	0.00	0.00	0	0.000	-1.00	0	0.000	0.00
TOTAL NON-CURRENT LIABILITIES	20,662	0.03	32,853	0.036	0.59	24,687	0.03	-0.25	27,671	0.032	0.12	19,372	0.022	-0.30
TOTAL LIABILITIES	66,485	0.10	84,216	0.092	0.27	118,037	0.16	0.40	141,716	0.166	0.20	175,290	0.200	0.24
PATRIMONY														
Social Capital	1,627	0.00	1,733	0.002	0.07	1,733	0.00	0.00	1,733	0.002	0.00	1,733	0.002	0.00
Capital Surplus	17,406	0.03	91,383	0.100	4.25	20,199	0.03	-0.78	20,199	0.024	0.00	20,199	0.023	0.00
Reservations	69,339	0.10	102,293	0.112	0.48	134,679	0.18	0.32	163,655	0.192	0.22	175,555	0.200	0.07
Equity revaluation	69,978	0.10	106,609	0.116	0.52	161,150	0.21	0.51	191,377	0.224	0.19	226,379	0.258	0.18
Revaluation of assets	62,851	0.09	68,262	0.075	0.09	71,119	0.09	0.04	58,695	0.069	-0.17	42,858	0.049	-0.27
Surplus of appraisals	387,607	0.58	461,531	0.504	0.19	245,104	0.33	-0.47	275,452	0.323	0.12	34,314	0.267	-0.15
TOTAL EQUITY	608,808	0.90	831,811	0.908	0.37	633,984	0.84	-0.24	711,111	0.834	0.12	701,038	0.800	-0.01
TOTAL LIABILITIES AND EQUITY	675,293	100.3%	916,027	100.0%	0.36	752,021	100.0%	-0.18	852,827	100.0%	0.13	876,328	100.0%	0.03

HERYO

INCOME STATEMENT
January 1 to December 31
(Amounts Expressed in millions of Colombian pesos)

	1996	%Part.	1997	%Part.	1998	%Part.	1999	%Part.	2000	% Part.
Operating Income	285,757	1.00	340,992	100%	402,736	100%	488,544	100%	572,086	100%
Cost of Sales	-210,639	-0.74	-245,738	-0.72	-294,272	-0.73	-348,091	-0.71	-415,635	-0.73
Operating Income Gross Profit	75,118	0.26	95,254	0.28	108,464	0.27	140,453	0.29	156,451	0.27
Operating Expenses Sales	-40,792	-0.14	-52,886	-0.16	-61,373	-0.15	-82,977	-0.17	-94,784	-0.17
Operating Expenses of Directors	-12,620	-0.04	-15,448	-0.05	-16,994	-0.04	-24,214	-0.05	-19,889	-0.03
Industrial and Commercial	21,706	0.08	26,920	0.08	30,097	0.07	33,262	0.07	41,778	0.07
Non-operating income:										
Dividends and Financial	12,198	0.04	13,496	0.04	16,336	0.04	18,463	0.04	18,367	0.03
Appreciation of Marketable					6,133	0.02	8,988	0.02	473	0.00
Gain on sale of investments and eq pp	14,434	0.05	23,035	0.07	10,322	0.03	8,648	0.02	806	0.00
Recoveries	6,906	0.02	3,570	0.01	5,820	0.01	276	0.00	1,053	0.00
Inflation Adjustments	9,371	0.03	9,172	0.03	12,592	0.03	1,632	0.00	2,582	0.00
Other	1,913	0.01	2,461	0.01	2,510	0.01	4,404	0.01	4,213	0.01
Total Non-operating income:	44,822	0.16	51,734	0.15	53,713	0.13	42,411	0.09	27,494	0.05
Non-operating expenses:										
Financial	-4,317	-0.02	-17,915	-0.05	-16,377	-0.04	-14,991	-0.03	-10,073	-0.02
Devaluation of marketable securities					-1,411	0.00	-2,040	0.00	-10,442	-0.02
Investment Protection Provision	-15,076	-0.05	-8,973	-0.03	-4,812	-0.01	-2,423	0.00	44	0.00
Other	-2,294	-0.01	-2,631	-0.01	-3,830	-0.01	-4,393	-0.01	-4,522	-0.01
Total Non-operating expenses:	-21,687	-0.08	-29,519	-0.09	-26,430	-0.07	-23,847	-0.05	-25,081	-0.04
Total non-operating income and expenses:	23,135	0.08	22,215	0.07	27,283	0.07	18,564	0.04	2,413	0.00
Utility of income tax	44,841	0.16	49,135	0.14	57,380	0.14	51,826	0.11	4,826	0.01
Income Tax	-1,440	-0.01	-2,086	-0.01	-6,441	-0.02	-5,900	-0.01	-12,036	-0.02
Net income before applying the Part Met	43,401	0.15	47,049	0.14	50,939	0.13	45,926	0.09	-7,210	-0.01
Income Equity Method	19,450	0.07	21,213	0.06	20,180	0.05	12,769	0.03	10,703	0.02
Net Income	62,851	0.22	68,262	0.20	71,119	0.18	58,695	0.12	3,493	0.01
Earnings per share *	773		788.0		821		677		495	

INDICADORES FINANCIEROS

		1996	1997	1998	1999	2000
A. LIQUIDITY						
Working Capital	D12-D35	37,960	29,744	15,709	25,753	2,194
Current ratio	D12/D35	1.8 Times	1.6 Times	1.2 Times	1.2 Times	1 Times
Acid Test	(D12-D10)/D35	1.1 Times	0.8 Times	0.6 Times	0.7 Times	0.6 Times
B. ACTIVITY						
Inventory Turnover	D63/D10	5.9 Times	6.1 Times	5.8 Times	5.9 Times	5.9 Times
Term average inventory	365/D106	62 Days	60 Days	63 Days	62 Days	62 Days
cxc rotation	D62/D9	6.9 Times	10.3 Times	8.4 Times	7 Times	7.7 Times
cxc-term average	365/D108	53 Days	35 Days	43 Days	52 Days	47 Days
CXP rotation	D62/(D29+D30)	9 Times	10.9 Times	4.8 Times	5.3 Times	5 Times
CxP average term	365/D110	41 Days	33 Days	77 Dias	68 Days	73 Days
active rotation	D62/D24	0.4 Times	0.4 Times	0.5 Times	0.6 Times	0.7 Times
C. ENDUDAMIENTO						
Debt Ratio (%) D43/D24		0.1	0.1	0.2	0.2	0.2
Reason liabilities of Capital (%) D42/D52		0.1	0.1	0.1	0.1	0.1
Debt Capital Index (%) (D42)/(D42+D52)		0.0	0.0	0.0	0.0	0.0
D. COVERAGE						
There are not enough data.						
E. PROFITABILITY						
Gross margin (%)	D64/D62	37.6	47.7	54.3	70.3	78.2
Net profit margin (%)	D89/D62	31.5	34.2	35.6	29.4	1.7
Investment Performance (%)	D89/D52	0.2	0.1	0.3	0.2	0.0
Profit Potential (%)	D89/D24	0.1	0.1	0.1	0.1	0.0
OTHER INDICATORS						
Relationship Property (%)	D52/D24	0.9	0.9	0.8	0.8	0.8
Rotation. D62/D99,2		7.50	11.50	25.60	19.00	260.80

CHAPTER 12

STATE OF SOURCES AND APPLICATIONS OF FUNDS

by josavere

INTRODUCTION

If the executive has more elements of judgment, probability make the right guess in the planning, execution, control and diagnosis of any situation to the financier. As the sailor takes a compass to guide the ship, the management must tell on a precede-established plan that takes shape with projected financial statements:result statement, general balance sheet, source and application of funds, projection of cash flow and projection of changes in the equity.

As a complement, all the prognoses are due to prepare that basic support the financial statements and with special care, the projection of cash flow, the most important financial tool in the short term, because it is the mathematical end result of integration of the budgets of sales, production, raw materials, costs of manufacture, expenses of administration and sales, investments, and the ability to be capitalized like, research and development, qualification, publicity, etc.

In this chapter, a very schematic presentation comes out of the projection of basic financial statements, because with them, the preparation of a masterful plan of value generation takes shape. In a previous chapter, we saw that is a requirement to clearly understand the processing of the statement of resources and application of funds.

1. PROJECTED RESULT STATEMENT

a. Sales: projected figures, considering the changes of prices in the prefixed dates; obviously talking about net sales.

b. Cost of sold merchandise: base on the set of inventories, the values projected for the raw materials and the precede-established policies by the management. It is worth the trouble to write down what's going to be the financial planning; it's recommendable always to work with the direct cost, system that facilitates the making of the decision. In addition, the high costs incurred by inefficiency, expenses of administration and sales, and other expenses are due to inform, and, in addition, correlating them with the operation level and prepared budgets to take care of the demand.

c. Financial expenses: calculated after processing the projection of the cash flow. It is an excellent tool to study different alternatives using the spreadsheet.

d. Taxes: for its calculation, we must consider the specific conditions of the particular company and the effective tributary legislation.

By arithmetic we arrived at the expected profit, amount that is going to be rejected in the equity increase, in the generation of funds and that constitutes a short term goal for the management. Let us remember that the objectives of the management must be long term, to avoid that the stability of the company/ for the sake of an immediate result is sacrificed.

Long-term handling obeys more to general policies than to mathematical approaches and, therefore, it demands a greater quota of responsibility and maturity on the part of the management. In addition to the EVACp, good tools for the handling of the long term, there are towing other basic statements, whose preparation we illustrated in a brief way.

2. PROJECTED GENERAL BALANCE SHEET

A. CURRENT ASSETS

a. Cash and banks: the figure leaves the final balance that is obtained with the projection of the cash flow.

b. Accounts receivable: adding to the initial balance, the sales on credit and reducing the considered collections (obviously, considering the recovery of slow portfolio and the possible delays of the period in which they are being budgeted).

c. Inventories: it is recommendable to separate the set in raw materials, products in process and finished, in the case of manufacturing companies. It is coming in the same way that in accounts to receive, but considering the amount of budgeted final inventory according to the policy drawn up.

d. Temporary investments: the data is obtained from the projection of cash flow.

e. Other current assets: it is coming from a similar way as the previous headings.

f. Fixed assets: to the initial set the amount defined in the budget of investments is added to it. Accrued depreciation calculates adding to the initial number the calculation for the period projected according to the method that the company uses to depreciate and considering the possible sale of assets.

B. LIABILITIES: as much for the balances of short as of long term the calculation is still simpler than for the assets, because these are characterized to have adelaide. The estimated is reduced to a problem of sum and subtractions.

Special care should be taken of one which has to do with the labor liabilities, which are due to consider base on the legal regime, or in the company policies. The actual calculation will give us a projection of the labor liabilities as far as retirement pensions, in case they appear in a company individually.

C. EQUITY: regarding to the tried schematizing we could speak of the obtaining of the equity figures by difference between assets and total liabilities. Of course, the discrimination of the equity is more recommendable considering the number of waited for, resulting profit of the projected statement of gains and losses and the policies of the company as far as dividends, the restrictions of the legal type and the thought of the management.

3. STATEMENT OF RESOURCES AND APPLICATION OF FUNDS

After having the projection of the result statement and the general balance sheet, we are in conditions to considering the statement of resources and application of cash.

Let us clarify that in this chapter the statement of resources and application of cash, has an approach strictly financial and non-accountable and for this reason we should leave that to the accountant. This tool will tells us where the cash was obtained from and how was it used.

It responds to a very common question but whose answer is not as simple as for example: what became of the cash of the sale of the land, why doesn't it pay dividends? Why does the company lose its capital? etc.

The companies enter effective by different aspects and all the cash arrive at the same funds where they lose the identity with a specific project. Although in the balance sheet in which the equity sets like legal reserve, for capitalization, future extensions, etc., it does not mean that the cash is in a certain banks, corporation or a safe. The cash is invested in the different headings from the assets. The statement of resource and application of funds outlines this explanation.

The **resources** are all increases of liabilities or to all decreases of assets. By deduction, **applications** are the increase of assets or the decreases of liabilities. Depreciation, although it does not constitutes income of cash, treats as a resource, since it refunds the set deducted in the statement of gains and losses, as an element of the cost of the sold merchandise, concretely as part of the general expenses of manufacture and that internally groups with the profit in the so called generated funds, or by the operations.

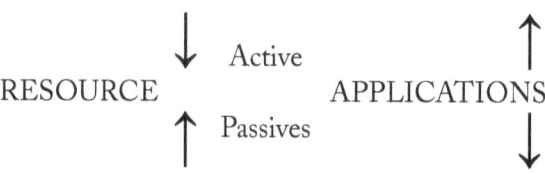

Regarding to the principle of company in progress and the inflationary phenomenon, the companies require every day more work capital to take care of the projected increase of operations. The prognosis of the cash flow indicates to us the additional requirements of the capital of work. Thus we must take the programming thus:

$$CT_2 = AC_2 - PC_2$$

$$CT1 = AC_1 - PC_1$$

Reducing $CT_2 - CT_1$

$$D\ CT = CT_2 - CT_1 = [(AC_2 - PC_2) - (AC_1 - PC_1)]$$

CT: capital of work projected period (2), bases (1)
AC: current assets projected period (2), base (1)
PC: current liabilities projected period (2), base (1)
D CT = required increase of the capital of work

Once determined the work capital (D CT), the financial planning begins properly as follows.

How one does prepares the state of resource and application of funds?

a. The additional needs of capital of work to be settle down that is required (D CT), should start off in the right column of the balance sheet; the resources with the applications. In a certain way we can simplify this as: the cash that the company must invest for the next period to keep growing.

b. The awaited changes in the other items that needs to be calculated, those that are not included in the capital of work. Applying the previously indicated guide we can tell if the change is a resource or an application.

c. The Statement sheet is prepared into two columns: to the left, **resources** and to the right, **applications**.

d. We need to the analyze emphasizing in the application of the financial **principle of compliance** and later, on the defined plan that is to be followed to indicate any oriented actions to increase the value generation.

$$CW + FA \cong P + LTP + PP$$

Example:

CONSOLIDATED STATE OF CHANGES IN THE FINANCIAL SITUATION

BALANCE SHEET
WWWW

	P0	P1	Differences	Source application
ACTIVE				
CURRENT ASSETS				
available	8.000.000	6.800.000	-1.200.000	source
investment	6.000.000	4.800.000	-1.200.000	source
x accounts receivable	80.000.000	62.825.000	-17.175.000	source
inventory				
raw material	640.000	556000 product		
in process	6.400.000	5.560.000		
finished product	24.000.000	20.870.000		
subtotal inventories	31.040.000	26.986.000	-4.054.000	source
Deferred	10.000.000	7.500.000	-2.500.000	source
Total current assets	135.040.000	108.911.000		
NON-CURRENT ASSETS				
Debtors	4.800.000	3.900.000	-900.000	source
property plant and equipment				
field	100.000.000	100000000 building		
	200.000.000	200.000.000		
machinery and equipment	160.000.000	160.000.000		
computing machinery	60.000.000	60.000.000		
vehicles	100.000.000	100.000.000		
Accumulated depreciation	-138.000.000	-148.000.000		
property plant subtotal and equipment	482.000.000	472.000.000	-10.000.000	source
Property Appreciation plant and equipment	800.000	685.000	-115.000	source
investment	45.000.000	33.215.000	-11.785.000	source
Investment Appreciation	24.200.000	17.100.000	-7.100.000	source
intangibles	7.000.000	4.800.000	-2.200.000	source
Other assets	141.000.000	98.850.000	-42.150.000	source
Appreciation Other assets	7.000.000	14.920.000	7.920.000	application
Total non-current assets	711.800.000	655.470.000		
TOTAL ASSETS	846.840.000	754.381.000		

LIABILITIES

LIABILITIES
CURRENT

financial obligations	55,000,000	48,245,000	-6,755,000	application
dividends payable	48,000,000	44,000,000	-4,000,000	application
suppliers	30,000,000			
foreign suppliers	3,000,000	27,900,000	24,900,000	source
Accounts Payable	25,420,000	22,495,000	-2,925,000	
rates	implementing tax liens		7,800,000	
job duties	7,500,000	-300		aplicación
estimated liabilities and provisions	44,000,000	40,740,000	-3,260,000	application
Deferred	9,000,000	7,500,000	-1,500,000	application
Total current liabilities	20,000,000	14,814,000	-5,186,000	application
NON-CURRENT LIABILITIES	**242,220,000**	**213,194,000**		
financial obligations				
job duties				
estimated liabilities and	56,000,000	50,122,000	-5,878,000	application
provisions	23,000,000	21,296,000	-1,704,000	application
Deferred	18,000,000	15,652,000	-2,348,000	application
Total non-current liabilities	15,000,000	13,513,000	-1,487,000	application
TOTAL LIABILITIES	**112,000,000**	**100,583,000**		

HERITAGE

social capital	175,000,000	162,500,000	-12,500,000	application
capital surplus	47,000,000	42,000,000	-5,000,000	application
Reservations	98,000,000	82,352,000	-15,648,000	application
reassessment of heritage	121,438,000	109,403,000	-12,035,000	application
Net income previous	19,182,000	16,524,000	-2,658,000	application
superhabit by valuations	32,000,000	27,825,000	-4,175,000	application
TOTAL ASSETS	**492,620,000**	**492,620,000**		
TOTAL LIABILITIES + HERITAGE	**846,840,000**	**806,397,000**		

Finance for Non-Financiers 1

SOURCES OF SHORT TERM		SHORT-TERM APPLICATIONS	
available	1,200,000	financial obligations	6,755,000
investment	1,200,000	dividends payable	4,000,000
x accounts receivable	17,175,000	suppliers	5,100,000
subtotal inventories	4,054,000	Accounts Payable	2,925,000
Deferred	2,500,000	tax liens and	300000
TOTAL	**26,129,000**	job duties	3,260,000
		estimated liabilities and provi	1,500,000
		Deferred	
		TOTAL	**29,026,000**

SOURCES OF LONG TERM		LONG-TERM APPLICATIONS	
Debtors	900000		
property, plant subtotal and equipment	10,000,000	other assets valuation	7920000
		financial obligations	5878000
		job duties	1704000
Property Appreciation plant and equipment	115000	estimated liabilities and provi	2348000
		Deferred	1487000
investment	11,785,000	reassessment of the heritage	12035000
Investment Appreciation	7,100,000	ant net income	2658000
intangibles	2,200,000	revaluation surplus	4175000
Other assets	42,150,000	capital surplus	5000000
TOTAL	**74,250,000**	social capital	12500000
		Reservations	15648000
TOTAL SOURCES	**100,379,000**	**TOTAL**	71353000
NET WORKING CAPITAL		**TOTAL APPLICATION**	100379000

CURRENT ASSETS—CURRENT LIABILITIES	-104283000

www.ingramcontent.com/pod-product-compliance
Lightning Source LLC
Chambersburg PA
CBHW030842180526
45163CB00004B/1423